William L. Keese

John Keese, Wit and Litterateur

Biographical Memoir

William L. Keese

John Keese, Wit and Litterateur
Biographical Memoir

ISBN/EAN: 9783743335288

Manufactured in Europe, USA, Canada, Australia, Japa

Cover: Foto ©ninafisch / pixelio.de

Manufactured and distributed by brebook publishing software (www.brebook.com)

William L. Keese

John Keese, Wit and Litterateur

JOHN KEESE,

WIT AND LITTÉRATEUR.

A BIOGRAPHICAL MEMOIR.

BY
WILLIAM L. KEESE.

NEW YORK:
D. APPLETON AND COMPANY,
1, 3, AND 5 BOND STREET.
1883.

COPYRIGHT BY
WILLIAM L. KEESE.
1883.

THIS MEMOIR
IS
LOVINGLY INSCRIBED
TO
MY MOTHER.

PREFACE.

MORE than a quarter of a century has passed since the death of the subject of the following pages; and few, if any, of those who were his intimates in other days are now living. Yet lively traditions of him remain among the book-selling fraternity, and it has been a matter of regret with many that his name does not appear in any American biographical dictionary.

In August, 1877, the late Evert A. Duyckinck contributed to the "Magazine of American History" an appreciative and entertaining paper entitled "Keeseana"—being his recollections of my father—in which he feelingly said that "Keese should not pass out of memory with the recollections of his many friends of the present fleeting generation." This paper was supplemented in the same year by a brief sketch by the present writer, in the same periodical; and in 1880 the late Henry Morford wrote and published, in the magazine bearing his name, a sketch of greater length entitled "John Keese; his Intimates," etc. These various writings were, naturally, all more or less of a fragmentary character, and did not pretend to an extended treatment of their subject.

The present composition is prepared with material gathered from many sources, and is designed to form a suitable biographical memoir. Surely a man whose life's aim was the diffusion of knowledge; whose name was identified with many important literary undertakings; and whose fame as an auctioneer was beyond doubt unique—deserves a record more enduring than memory.

W. L. K.

April, 1883.

MEMOIR.

JOHN KEESE, the subject of the present memoir, was born in the city of New York, November 24, 1805, and was the second son of William Keese and Rebecca Linn. His father was a lawyer of reputation, and his license of admission to the bar (now lying before me) bears the signature of James Kent. His mother was a daughter of the Rev. William Linn, D. D., a native of Pennsylvania, one of the most eloquent divines of his time, first Chaplain of the House of Representatives of the United States, under the Constitution of 1787, and celebrated as a pulpit orator in New York during the last decade of the last century.

Mr. Keese had reason to be proud of his grandfathers. John Keese, the father of William Keese, was also by profession a lawyer; became assistant deputy quartermaster-general on Washington's staff, and was one of the original members of the Society of the Cincinnati. The Rev. William Linn enjoyed the high honor of being chosen to deliver before the Society of the Cincinnati the oration on the death of General Washington, the effort, as it is recorded, " placing him notably beyond his pulpit compeers of that day." I view it in the light of a striking coincidence that one grandfather should have been a listener to an oration pronounced by the other before the renowned society on so solemn and impressive an occasion; and I am sure that the grandson ever proudly cherished such honored ancestral memories.

The bright intelligence of Mr. Keese was early apparent, and it was decided in family council to educate him for the ministry. At his father's death, however, it seemed expedient, if not, indeed, necessary, that he should enter on a mercantile career; and, on being asked his preference in that regard, declared it earnestly for the book business, thus revealing that predilection for letters which led him into the walks of literature; incited him to persistent self-culture; gained him the acquaintance and friendship of men of genius; and proved in the end a consolation for the loss of collegiate honors.

It may be proper to mention here that a later family conclave decreed that the eldest brother should espouse the Church, and accordingly William Linn Keese became a clergyman of the Episcopal faith, a devoted follower of Christ, an eloquent divine, loved and honored as a man and pastor in the communities where he lived and taught.

About the year 1823, at the age of eighteen, Mr. Keese entered as clerk the book and publishing house of Collins & Hannay, located in Pearl Street; and after years of faithful service was admitted to a partnership (about 1836), under the new firm-name of Collins, Keese & Co., which firm continued until 1842, when it was dissolved by mutual consent. He then formed a co-partnership with James E. Cooley and Horatio Hill, in the book-auction business, under the firm-name of Cooley, Keese & Hill; and, subsequently, through the retirement of Mr. Hill, Cooley & Keese, which association continued to 1853 or 1854, when the firm was dissolved, and Mr. Keese obtained the appointment of Appraiser of Books in the New York Custom-House, which position he filled until his death, his spare evenings being employed, when health permitted, in his vocation of auctioneer. A severe bronchial affection, from which he had long been a sufferer, was the precursor to pulmonary consumption, and of that malady he died on the 30th of May, 1856, at the age of fifty years and six months.

He married in 1832 Elizabeth Willets, daughter of Zebulon S. Willets. Nine children were born to them, of whom six and their mother are still living. Three are no more. Jonathan Lawrence, the eldest of the children, died, in the flower of his youth, of a wound received from the accidental discharge of a musket, while a member of the Seventh Regiment, at Camp Cameron, in 1861; * Willets, the third child, perished

---

* "On the 9th of May, Private J. Larrie Keese, of the Eighth Company, was killed by the accidental discharge of a musket. As this was the first death in the regiment, and Keese was a young man of excellent business, social, and literary abilities, and a general favorite, gloom was cast over the camp. Appropriate resolutions were passed by his comrades, and a sergeant and six men were detailed by the colonel to accompany the remains, in their

by drowning in 1843; and Edmund Willets, the eighth child, died in infancy.

Throughout his career, Mr. Keese lost no opportunity for improving his mind and adding to his intellectual resources. The academic education he had received kindled his ambition, while it left him with wistful gaze bent on unexplored regions of knowledge; and he sought in books a consolation for the university curriculum denied him by circumstance. He read almost omnivorously, and the gift of a singularly retentive memory aided essentially in the process of self-cultivation. Nor did the knowledge thus gained suffer from stagnation. Whatever learning was his, circulated freely. He possessed an imaginative mind; his perception was acute; he was "witty and full of invention"; his taste was catholic; he was eminently companionable, and an admirable conversationalist; and when, subsequently, he was drawn naturally into the society of book-men and men of letters, where there was no lack of mental friction, he contributed his full share to the intellectual commerce of the hour. He loved to impart whatever he knew of interest or desert; he treasured up good

---

metallic coffin, to Brooklyn. In the latter city, imposing and impressive funeral ceremonies were held at Christ Church by Rev. Dr. Canfield, and a throng of five thousand citizens came to pay the last rites of respect to the first of the long list of hero-martyrs that the Seventh Regiment was destined to furnish to the country. The *cortège*, preceded by an escort of the National Guard Reserve Corps and two platoons of the Ninth Regiment, and many military guests, proceeded to Greenwood Cemetery, where Keese was buried with military honors."—(" History of the Seventh Regiment," by WILLIAM SWINTON, A. M.)

things for his friends; and his fluent speech was enriched with illustrations born of his varied and well-remembered reading. In brief, the arms of his mental arsenal were constantly shouldered, aimed, and fired! Many a man of infinitely greater culture has made less of an impression by his attainments. He was not a man of extensive erudition; not a classical scholar; nothing of a linguist. He knew something of the Greek and Latin authors through translations; in the same way of French and Italian literature; but there his knowledge in that direction ended. He was, indeed, familiar with the English classics; with the great body of English and American literature; and especially with the poetry of both countries; but this familiarity was due, not to the studious, painstaking application necessary to form the panoply of a college professor, but to a loving and appreciative course of reading in hours of leisure. It was not his fault that his mother-wit, his memory, and his intellectual readiness, combined, unconsciously to himself, to convey the impression of a scholarship greater than he had the good fortune to possess.

In 1832 he was a member, and later the "Speaker," of "The Column," a literary association then flourishing in the city,* and numbering on its roll many

---

* The Column Club still exists, and dined at Pinard's last spring. From an account of the dinner, published in the "New York World" the day after, the following details are extracted:

"In the year 1826 twenty young men organized a debating society in this city, which met once a week at the residence of some member of the society. The momentous questions debated were such that, were they now discussed

names that became more or less distinguished—such as Anthony Robertson, Jonathan Nathan, John Gourlie, Oliver Strong, and Augustus Schell. A society so congenial to his tastes could not fail to develop his proclivities, while it afforded a field for their exercise; and it was here, no doubt, that his fluency of speech, facility of retort, and sparkling wit, first became apparent as clearly defined mental characteristics; and their recognition speedily advanced him to the speakership, and into gratifying popularity.

The orations and speeches of famous orators and

---

in Congress, the United States would be promptly plunged into war with every nation on earth. Each question was put to a vote, and in case of a tie the president at once, by his casting vote, decided, for example, 'whether England was justified or not in incarcerating Napoleon.' Finally, the debates became so very animated that no one would allow the club to meet in his private house, and the Rev. Dr. Lyell, rector of Christ Church, then on Anthony Street, now Worth Street, gave them the use of a small room at the back of the church. At that time the church was considered to be almost out of town, so that the eloquent orators could not disturb the quiet of the city. In the center of the room was a column to support the roof, and, as the club had no name, the Rev. Dr. Lyell suggested that it be called the 'Column Club' until the last member passed away. When the church was remodeled, shortly after, Judge Robertson gave the club the use of an attic in his palatial residence on that then fashionable and aristocratic thoroughfare, Leonard Street. The club was then nicknamed the 'Attic Club.' Judge Robertson soon found that he had made a very poor bargain, and drove them out. In 1828 they secured the loft of the old sugar-house which stood on the corner of Broadway and Leonard Street, and here for many years subsequently they held forth to their own great satisfaction, but not to the peace of the Commonwealth of New York. Among those who have been foremost in the debates, and who are still in active life among us, are Mr. William M. Evarts, Mr. Hamilton Fish, Mr. Augustus Schell, Mr. John Bigelow, Mr. Edward S. Van Winkle, Mr. John H. Gourlie, Mr. Parke Godwin, Mr. William M. Pritchard, Mr. George B. Butler, Mr. George H. Hoffman, and Dr. Alonzo Clarke, all of whom dined last night at Pinard's, except Mr. Bigelow (who is abroad), and talked over their early days."

statesmen had a great attraction for him, and he was familiar with all recorded celebrated rhetorical efforts. Many passages of eloquence and beauty he retained in memory, and was never tired of repeating them. How well I remember the first time he recited to me an extract from the speech of Lord Brougham on law reform, containing the famous antitheses: "It was the boast of Augustus—it formed part of the glare in which the perfidies of his earlier years were lost—that he found Rome of brick, and left it of marble; a praise not unworthy a great prince, and to which the present reign also has its claims. But how much nobler will be the sovereign's boast, when he shall have it to say that he found law dear, and left it cheap; found it a sealed book—left it a living letter; found it the patrimony of the rich—left it the inheritance of the poor; found it the two-edged sword of craft and oppression—left it the staff of honesty and the shield of innocence!"

Then he loved to recall a striking figure made by Rufus Choate, in an oration he heard him deliver in New York, in which figure the Empire City, commanding tribute from land and water, was thus finely pictured: Drawing himself to his full height and extending both arms, the orator exclaimed, "With one hand she grasps the teeming harvests of the West, and with the other, like Venice, weds the everlasting sea!"

Extracts from the speeches of Chatham, Pitt, Burke, Fox, Sheridan, Grattan, Erskine, Curran, Calhoun, Webster, Clay, he could repeat at will; and the writer owes many an hour of delightful instruction to accounts, made vivid by quotation, of the efforts of those illustrious men.

A little volume of the addresses delivered by Dr. Nott, at Union College, to the candidates for the baccalaureate, was an especial favorite; and, as now I turn its leaves, his admiration and fondness for those glowing and lofty discourses are remembered. I pause to quote the following passage from one of the addresses, as serving to indicate the character of an eloquence that so affected him; and one can fancy how powerfully swayed must have been the doctor's listeners:

"I have often, young gentlemen, recommended to you a sacred adherence to truth. I would on this occasion repeat the recommendation, that I may fix it the more indelibly on your hearts. Believe me, when I tell you that on this article you can never be too scrupulous. Truth is one of the fairest attributes of Deity. It is the boundary which separates vice from virtue—the line which divides heaven from hell. It is the chain which binds the man of integrity to the throne of God, and, like the God to whose throne it binds him, till this chain is dissolved, his word may be relied on. Suspended on this, your property, your reputation, your life, are safe. But against the malice of a liar there is no security. He can be bound by nothing. His soul is already repulsed to an immeasurable distance from that Divinity a sense of whose presence is the security of virtue. He has sundered the last of those moral ligaments which bind a mortal to his duty. And having done so, through the extended region of fraud and falsehood, without a bond to check or a limit to confine him, he ranges, the dreaded enemy of innocence; whose lips pollute even truth itself as it passes through them, and whose breath, like the pestilential mists of hades, blasts, and soils, and poisons as it touches."

He greatly admired the speeches made by Kossuth, during his visit as the guest of the nation in 1851; and I seem to hear his enthusiastic praise of the patriot's eloquence, so clear is the recollection of how it stirred and impressed him.

As in those of prose, Mr. Keese was as rich in treasures of poetry. His memory was stored with gems of verse, easily summoned to embellish a speech, to supply a poetic image, to furnish an instance of beauty, and to entertain.*

He was fond of reciting to his children, and I well remember the effect produced by his recitation in the family circle one evening of Byron's "Prisoner of Chil-

---

* The late Mr. Henry Morford, in an appreciative sketch published in 1880, refers as follows to Mr. Keese's entertaining versatility: " Not second even to Mr. Keese's wit, in the ordinary understanding of that word, was his really wondrous talent for improvisation. At no time did it seem difficult for him to take up magazine or newspaper, and read from it a page or column, not one word of which existed in print, and yet so perfect in composition that no one could fail to be deceived until after-examination of the sheet showed the trick; and what could go nearer to the very highest honors claimed for the Italian *improvisatores?* His reading aloud was almost as marvelous as the last accomplishments named. Nearly forty years have not dimmed, in the mind of the writer, the recollection of having first heard him read Longfellow's 'Skeleton in Armor,' then just published, the 'Ancient Mariner,' 'Christabel,' and some of the finer passages of Shelley, Scott, Byron, and others of the English classics."

lon"—our first acquaintance with that fascinating poem. All through—the description of the brothers; the one whose

>". . . soul was of that mold
> Which in a palace had grown cold,
> Had his free breathing been denied
> The range of the steep mountain's side"—

and he

>". . . the favorite and the flower,
> Most cherished since his natal hour,
> His mother's image in fair face,
> The infant love of all his race"—

their death, and the last brother's agony and swoon— the lovely bird that came to his grated window—the slow-dragging years:

>"At last men came to set me free,
> I asked not why, and recked not where;
> It was at length the same to me,
> Fettered or fetterless to be—
> I learned to love despair"—

all this, the pathos and eloquence of the narrative, affected us in no small degree, and many succeeding weeks found me engaged in committing the poem to memory.

There was another poem he used to recite to us, and we shall never forget the effect it produced. It was the story of a poor, half-witted boy, who lived alone with his mother, a widow. She died, and he followed silently when she was borne to the grave. Left there, and incapable of realizing the fact of death, he opens the grave, bears home the corse, kindles anew the fire, and endeavors to reanimate the lifeless form. This poem we often listened to, and I once wrote it down from memory; but was never sure of my recollection. I could never find it in any book of selections, and never knew who was the author. Some years ago, I encountered it for the first time in print, in Forney's "Anecdotes of Public Men," as having been recited by Edwin Forrest with surpassing effect at a gathering of friends in Mr. Forney's rooms at Washington, some time between the years 1860 and 1871. Mr. Forney says, in alluding to Forrest's splendid contribution to the evening's entertainment, "But nothing that he did will be remembered longer than the manner in which he recited 'The Idiot Boy,' a production up to that time unknown to everybody in the room except Forrest and myself, and to me only because I heard him repeat it seven years before."

Forney, having heard Forrest repeat it seven years prior to the occasion quoted (probably 1861), would make his knowledge of it date from 1854; but I remember hearing the poem from my father long before that, so it was not unknown to him. And now, since so much has been said about a composition that certainly was distinguished by association, it may be of interest to our readers to see it for themselves. I copy the verses as given by Colonel Forney:

THE IDIOT BOY.

It had pleased God to form poor Ned
    A thing of idiot mind,
Yet, to the poor, unreasoning boy,
    God had not been unkind.

Old Sarah loved her helpless child,
    Whom helplessness made dear;
And he was everything to her,
    Who knew no hope or fear.

She knew his wants, she understood
    Each half-articulate call,
For he was everything to her,
    And she to him was all.

And so for many a year they lived,
    Nor knew a wish beside;
But age at last on Sarah came,
    And she fell sick—and died.

He tried in vain to waken her,
    He called her o'er and o'er;
And, when they told him she was dead,
    The words no import bore.

They closed her eyes and shrouded her,
    While he stood wondering by,
And, when they bore her to the grave,
    He followed silently.

They laid her in the narrow house,
    They sang the funeral stave;
And, when the funeral train dispersed,
    He lingered by that grave.

The rabble boys, that used to jeer
    Whene'er they saw poor Ned,
Now stood and watched him by the grave,
    And not a word they said.

They came and went and came again,
    Till night at last came on;
Yet still he lingered by the grave
    Till every one had gone.

And when he found himself alone,
    He swift removed the clay;
Then raised the coffin up in haste,
    And bore it swift away.

He bore it to his mother's cot,
    And laid it on the floor,
And with the eagerness of joy
    He barred the cottage door.

Then out he took his mother's corpse,
    And placed it in a chair;
And soon he heaped the hearth and made
    The kindling fire with care.

He had put his mother in *her* chair,
    And in its wonted place,
And then he blew the fire, which shone,
    Reflected in her face.

And, pausing now, her hand would feel,
And then her face behold:
"*Why*, mother, do you look so pale,
And why are you so cold?"

It had pleased God from the poor wretch
His only friend to call;
Yet God was kind to him, and soon
In death restored him all.

I have preserved a record of a booksellers' dinner—a "complimentary entertainment by the booksellers of New York to authors and other literary and distinguished men"—given at the City Hotel, March 30, 1837. This was over forty-five years ago, and few, if any, indeed, of the company then met are now living. Yet there may be descendants of some of them who will feel an interest in a scene where names familiar and dear to them appear.

David Felt presided on the occasion, assisted by Fletcher Harper and others as vice-presidents; George Dearborn, a well-known publisher, officiated as master-of-ceremonies, and Mr. Keese as toast-master. He had then been of the firm of Collins, Keese & Co. for more than a year, and his genial qualities had gained him many friends among the booksellers and publishers of New York and elsewhere.

Among the entertainers and guests were Albert Gallatin, Chancellor Kent, Colonel Trumbull, Washington Irving, William Cullen Bryant, Fitz-Greene Halleck, Rev. Orville Dewey, James K. Paulding, William L.

Stone, Harrison Gray, James Harper, Charles King, Major Noah, Philip Hone, John W. Francis, Lewis Gaylord Clark, George P. Morris, Edgar A. Poe, Richard Adams Locke, George P. Putnam, Henry Inman, J. G. Chapman, and many others.

The opening address, previous to introducing the regular toasts, was delivered by Mr. Keese; and, in the course of it, he spoke with much feeling of the occasion which had brought them together, and of the fraternal relation between author and publisher, which it was designed to foster and maintain for mutual benefit. Glancing at the progress of American literature, and viewing the animating prospect of the future, he said: "When we survey the geographical position of these United States—when we behold our vast region bounded by no diversity of language, and all its borders teeming with a reading community—we discover a wide field for the transmission of the literature of our countrymen. No nation on the face of the earth displays such peculiar advantages for the circulation and consumption of intellectual produce."

The following extract, in which Cooper, Kent, Irving, and Halleck were happily alluded to, was received with enthusiasm: "Sir, it is a well-known fact that the publishers in our principal cities have justly and munificently appreciated the intellect of our land, and her sons have shared largely with the bookseller in the profits derived from their literary labors. The historical and creative genius of one who is not inaptly termed 'our *pioneer* of mind'; the commentaries of our American Blackstone; the splendid sketches of our *own particular son* (who, greeted with the incense of foreign praise, has brought back to us a heart untraveled and a love for home), together with the works of gifted minds in every department of science, poesy, and fiction, all attest the liberality and enterprise of American publishers. We desire still further to explore the mind where mental ore lies buried, to awaken slumbering genius, and to call into active exercise the dormant energy and shrinking talent of our young and much-loved land. Why sleeps the Muse of Drake's twin-brother bard? Why comes not he forth with fairy wand to silence the scribblers of the day? Who among us would not esteem it a high honor to be his publisher, and to issue his beautiful creations in a guise as beautiful as the taste of our best artisans can exhibit?"*

The speech of the evening, in weight and importance, was delivered by William L. Stone, then senior of the editorial corps in New York city, in response to the toast of "The periodical press." It was noteworthy for its wealth of statistical information respecting book-publication, as well as for its vigorous and felicitous diction. A vein of scholarly erudition ran through it, and occasional touches of sprightly and fanciful humor saved it from any approach to prosiness.

There were speeches by Harrison Gray, James Harper, Charles King, Major Noah, Matthew L. Davis,

---

* Three years later, Mr. Keese made good his wish to present the productions of American mind, by the issue of his "Poets of America," "in a guise as beautiful" as the compilation deserved.

Chancellor Kent, Philip Hone, John W. Francis, Washington Irving, and James K. Paulding.

It may amuse a later generation of Franklin Square publishers to read the pleasant little speech made by one of their ancestors; and I hope they will enjoy it as much as his listeners did in 1837. In response to the toast, "The booksellers of New York," Mr. James Harper, being long and loudly called for, finally rose and observed: That he was at a loss to know why he should be singled out to respond to the compliment, as there were many of the trade present greatly his seniors. Besides, it was well known to his brethren that he was no orator—that it was entirely out of his line to make *speeches*—that he was simply a humble maker of *books*, and that this alone was his profession. Therefore, although the subject and the occasion were of a highly prolific character, still he should not attempt a speech on the occasion—for, if he should, he would assuredly find himself in the dilemma of a certain Massachusetts orator, who, while addressing a public assembly, unfortunately lost the thread of his discourse, and, hesitating to recover his lost ideas, was addressed from the gallery by a raw country lad, "*I say, Mister, I guess you're stuck.*" "And, Mr. President" (added Mr. Harper, after a pause), "so am I!"

Matthew L. Davis, in the course of a few remarks, said that being one of the oldest of those present who had been engaged in the manufacture of books, he recollected some interesting facts in the progress of the art; and mentioned as a remarkable contrast to its extent at that day, that about twenty years back, when an edition of Brown's "Commentary on the Bible" was projected in New York, the Legislature of the State passed, in both branches, a resolution recommending public patronage to the immense undertaking.

The speech of Dr. Francis called forth the warmest plaudits. It was full of humorous suggestion, and eminently characteristic of the man.

Washington Irving, in proposing the health of Samuel Rogers, the banker-poet, referred to a letter he had received the previous day from Mr. Rogers, acknowledging the receipt of a volume of Halleck's poems, and speaking of them in the highest terms. Of "Marco Bozzaris" and "Alnwick Castle," "They are better than anything we can do just now on our side of the Atlantic," said Rogers.

Letters were read from Fenimore Cooper, Nicholas Biddle, Edward Everett, Daniel Webster, Noah Webster, Gulian C. Verplanck, and many others.

Some of the toasts and sentiments were as follow:

From Noah Webster: "May booksellers honorably rival each other in the sale of good books, and may good books *find* or *make* good readers and good citizens!"

From N. P. Willis: "The republic of letters — in which all who speak the same language are compatriots, and should reciprocate protection and kind feeling."

By Lewis Gaylord Clark: "Protection to home manufactures, whether of the hands or of the intellect."

By Edgar A. Poe: "The monthlies of Gotham—

their distinguished editors and their vigorous collaborators."

By Fletcher Harper: "Booksellers—generous individuals, who kindly assist authors to obtain an immortality in which they themselves do not participate."

By George P. Putnam: "The female intellects of our country — brilliant luminaries in its literary horizon."

By John Keese: "The memory of Cadmus, the first postboy. He carried letters from Phœnicia to Greece."

Such was the occasion, interesting and memorable for those who participated in it so long ago, and it seems an old story to revive and print in this present year of grace. Yet there is a charm in any record of the past which bears the names of those who dying left an honored memory, or a rich legacy in their works; and as the gatherings of authors and men of letters have yielded haunting pages of literary history, so may this "Booksellers' Dinner" prove a welcome leaf, though pressed for so many years.

I confess, however, at the same time, to a wish to show the society and association enjoyed by Mr. Keese at this period, and to hint at the advantages and opportunities offered by such acquaintance and connections for social and commercial advancement. He profited greatly thereby; and that he was not unworthy of the friendships then begun, the continuance of the relation in sympathy and regard for long years thereafter sufficiently assures me.

Mr. Keese was a genuine Gothamite. He loved

New York as Sydney Smith loved London. It was the field *par excellence* for the development of social instinct, for intellectual expansion, and for interchange of ideas. The city's march in improvement and extent he watched with constant interest, and in her growing greatness felt a becoming pride. Yet his "down-town" apprenticeship had familiarized him with the old landmarks, and their effacement, consequent upon metropolitan advance, tinged his pride with regret at the loss of historic significance. I now recall how at a later date, when the question of opening a street through Trinity Church-yard was agitated, this feeling found expression in the following lines from a poem of local character, written for a literary society in which he was interested:

"The ancient grave-yard where our fathers sleep,
  Thus far's resisted innovation's sweep;
But sacrilegious hands would fain deface
The sacred soil that marks their resting-place.
The untutored Indian lingers by the mound;
His father's grave is consecrated ground;
And where old Trinity its grandeur rears,
Lies holy dust, hallowed by many tears.
Here sleeps the SAILOR from whose dying lip
Fell words immortal—'DON'T GIVE UP THE SHIP!'
The dust of HAMILTON reposes near;
New York's gray veterans are buried here;
Statesmen and warriors, holy men of God,
Manhattan's matrons, sleep beneath that sod.
Genius has hallowed many a moldering stone;
Here slept the patriot when his work was done;

Many lie here who welcomed freedom's birth—
Oh, spare their graves!—'tis consecrated earth;
Sacred from aught, save where the evening breeze
Sighs a sad requiem through swaying trees;
Sacred from sound, save where the deep-toned bell
O'er clustering graves repeats their funeral-knell,
Or calls the living to those early times
When those who rest there listened to those chimes.
Oh, let not Mammon's specious hands *improve*
A soil embalmed with tears of faith and love!
Let the world see that here there are some spots
Too sacred and too dear for 'building-lots.'
Let Speculation take another range,
Nor sell our fathers' bones at the Exchange!"

Mr. Keese was passionately fond of the drama, and witnessed the acting of all the great artists of his time. In early days, when clerking it on a modest salary, he often dispensed with a meal that he might have the wherewithal to buy a seat in the pit of the Old Park, during the engagement of Edmund Kean on his second visit to America in 1825. All the renowned actors whose names are associated with the "palmy days" of that famous theatre, he saw, and his recollections of their performances were vivid and interesting. He possessed a no small degree of mimetic power, and often entertained a social circle with imitations of celebrated actors, simulating voice, gesture, and method with surprising accuracy. A favorite effort was the tent-scene in "Richard III," after the manner of Kean, and it was thought to be a close approach to the style of the great tragedian. His admiration for Kean was boundless, and he was never tired of talking about him, and of describing the impression his acting produced on himself and others. He declared that he was so affected by the curse in Lear, that Kean's countenance —his trembling, imprecatory hands—for days after, were constantly before his eyes like a vision.

An instance of the imitative faculty spoken of created an amusing scene in the auction-room one evening, and I will introduce it here. The incident is related by Laurence Hutton, in his volume of "Plays and Players," and I give it in his own words:

"Of John Keese, a well-known auctioneer in New York during the past generation, the following auction-room story is still told: At a book-sale here during the first great 'Hunchback' excitement, while the Kembles were nightly appearing in the play, Mr. Keese knocked down two volumes to the bid of a mild little gentleman, who, upon being asked his name, replied faintly and frightenedly, 'Clifford!' Immediately striking the familiar attitude, Mr. Keese exclaimed, ' 'Tis Clifford's voice, if ever Clifford spoke!' and, after the storm of laughter which followed had subsided, and as the quiet gentleman, very much disconcerted, was hurrying from the room, he added, with all the pathetic intensity of Miss Kemble herself, 'Clifford, why *don't* you speak to me?'

"The sale was interrupted for many minutes. There was, perhaps, hardly a man in the room who was not as familiar with the tone and style of Miss Kemble, and with that particular scene in the play, as was Mr. Keese; and the applause he received was as hearty as ever encouraged the best *Julia* on the professional stage. Clifford never called to claim his books."

Mr. Keese would have made an excellent actor; and his dramatic aptitude and fondness for the stage led him sometimes to take part in private theatricals. One of those occasions may be briefly referred to. It was when an amateur representation of " The Rivals" was given, forty years ago, at New Brighton, Staten Island —then the city's most fashionable summer resort—by ladies and gentlemen of New York society, or, to borrow the phrase of the newspaper report, " by the fair daughters and wits of Gotham."

Private theatricals at that time were something of a novelty, and it was well known that unusual preparations had been made to present the comedy with becoming and artistic fitness. The progress of rehearsal had kindled anticipation, and the gay party at " The Pavilion" were in a flutter of excitement and delight at what promised to be in all respects the crowning event of the season.

At last the evening came, and with it a goodly host of friends and acquaintances from the metropolis. The spacious saloon of " The Pavilion" had been prepared and dressed for the occasion, and exhibited to the admiring audience a bewitching scene of refined and elegant adornment. Music, light, and fragrance contributed to augment the charm.

The affair was a complete success, and elicited enthusiastic plaudits. I can not vouch for the acting, but it was reported to have been excellent at all points. It is to be hoped that it was so, since the late Henry Placide, that rare comedian, was among the attentive auditors.

"At the fall of the curtain," says a record of the entertainment, "the audience, consisting of nearly five hundred persons, composed of the wealth, fashion, and beauty of New York, 'called out' the performers, who bowed their acknowledgments. Sir Lucius O'Trigger (Mr. Keese), however, was called on for a speech, and accordingly made the following appropriate remarks: 'On my conscience, ladies and gentlemen, I appear before you with more than my usual modest diffidence; for, although I see around me roses and tulips, blooming in *parterres*, we can boast too of one "sweet Dalia" behind the curtain, that, by my own blushes, would rival the brightest carnation among you. Most gratefully do I thank you, ladies and gentlemen, for the kind countenance and patient attention you have given to our amateur efforts this evening; and, although we have not been entirely "absolute" in our perfection, nor perhaps merited the kindness and consideration of such "acres" of friends, on my faith, we will never cease to be "Rivals."'"

He never lost his interest in the drama; and, indeed, it was given a new lease of life when, after William E. Burton established himself in Chambers Street, he became acquainted with that great actor. His old-time friend, the late lamented James T. Fields, in his pathetic sketch of reminiscence,* bore him thus in memory:

---

* "Then." "Harper's Magazine," August, 1881.

"Then John Keese, good-natured, merry soul, introduced us to Mr. Manager Mitchell and pretty Mary Taylor, behind the scenes at the small Olympic."

I now come to an important period in my father's career—that of editorship. It has been said that he was an ardent lover of poetry. The English poets he had read and was familiar with, and many of them had been subjects of diligent and appreciative study. His tenacious memory garnered as he read, and to the end of his life those rich resources were his to draw upon at any moment. And now a warm interest in the progress of American poetry awoke within him, and a survey of the garden of native song allured him to the loving task of gathering a garland of its flowers.

The first volume of the "Poets of America" was published in 1840. Edgar A. Poe, who, whatever may have been his faults in a critical capacity, and despite his rancorous tendency, was certainly competent to pass upon such a work, says, in his review of "Mr. Griswold and the Poets," after noticing the respective collections of Kettell, Cheever, Morris, and Bryant: "Mr. Keese succeeded much better. He brought to his task, if not the most rigorous impartiality, at least a fine taste, a sound judgment, and a more thorough acquaintance with our poetical literature than had distinguished either of his predecessors."

The lack of "rigorous impartiality" may have been owing to the fact that many of the writers whose names gave luster to the volume were held in personal esteem;

and friendly feeling, possibly, in a measure swayed the judgment; but, in any view, the compilation was really the first repository that could lay claim to being distinctly representative of native poetry, presented in an attractive form. " American poetry," says the editor's preface, " has hitherto been little more than a happy accident, and seems to have arisen in spite of the practical tendencies of our country and the prosaic character of our time. . . . It has usually come before the public eye in small, detached portions, with slight pretension to permanence in the form of its publication, and has been rescued from speedy oblivion only by its own beauty and power. The genius of the artist and the liberality of the publisher have done far too little toward presenting in an attractive shape and with due advantages the finest productions of our poets. We have left our pearls unstrung. We have made few attempts to heighten the brilliancy of our gems by the beauty of their setting."

No one will doubt the truth of these words who will consider for a moment how the popular taste for many years past has come to regard illustrations as an almost indispensable adjunct to collections of poetry; and that publishers are as truly alive to the importance of pictorial embellishment as they are to that of the text it adorns. It was, then, prophetic forecast to discern the needed element. The reading public was quick to recognize the delicate and graceful creations of the artist's pencil in " The Poets of America," and the work in two series passed through several editions, universally commended by the press, and admired by all lovers of poetry.*

The "Poetical Remains" of Miss Lucy Hooper, a young and gifted poetess of Brooklyn, in whose career

---

* The following editorial, under the heading of "Our Poets Forty-three Years ago," appeared in the Boston "Evening Transcript" of March 1, 1882 :

"It is worth while sometimes to look back on our past and see what it promised ; then to return to the present and see how those promises have been kept. In the realm of poetry, many have been realized, exceeding the most sanguine expectations of the author's best friends. We have before us a book bound in a fine, old-fashioned elegance, entitled 'The Poets of America: illustrated by one of her Painters,' edited by John Keese, and copyrighted by Samuel Colman, of New York, in 1839. In the preface the editor says : 'American poetry has hitherto been little more than a happy accident, and seems to have arisen in spite of the practical tendencies of our country and the prosaic character of our time. It has been produced mostly by minds devoted to sterner studies, and in brief intervals of leisure snatched from more engrossing toils. The intellectual energy of our land has as yet consecrated itself, perhaps too exclusively, to the mighty work of preparing a spacious home for the thronging multitudes of our population, and building up for their protection a great national polity. The main part of our poetical literature, therefore, has been occasional and fugitive. It has usually come before the public eye in small, detached portions, with slight pretension to permanence in the form of its publication, and has been rescued from speedy oblivion only by its own beauty and power. . . . Of the literary character of this work it is not necessary that the editor should speak. He has sought to present, in a fitting form, some of the finest specimens—the true spirit of American poetry ; and, if he has not failed in his attempt, the volume surely is worthy of perusal and preservation. He commends it, then, to the library and the boudoir. He trusts that the bright glance of the beautiful and the accomplished will always rest upon its pages with pleasure, and that even the sobriety of scholarship and the sternness of criticism will sometimes kindle into the enthusiasm of praise.'

"The birthday of our poet Longfellow brought this old book to mind, as he was one of those complimented by two selections in the eighty-eight 'specimens' from sixty-one different authors, a list of whom we annex. It will be a curiosity to many of our readers, and to many call up some precious memories:

"Allston, Bryant, Brooks, Barker, Burr, Bird, Cutter, Clarke, Drake Davidson, Dana, Doane, Dawes, Dinnies, Daponte, Everett, Ellet, Embury, he had taken a warm interest, were gathered and published with a memior in 1842; and the volume gained an added and tender grace in bearing the sweet and loving tribute of Whittier, commencing—

> "They tell me, Lucy, thou art dead—
> That all of thee we loved and cherished
> Has with thy summer roses perished;
> And left, as its young beauty fled,
> An ashen memory in its stead!
> Cold twilight of a parted day."

And ending—

> "All lovely things by thee beloved
> Shall whisper to our hearts of thee,
> These green hills where thy childhood roved,
> Yon river winding to the sea—
> The sunset light of autumn eves
> Reflecting on the deep, still floods,
> Cloud, crimson sky, and trembling leaves
> Of rainbow-tinted woods—
> These, in our view, shall henceforth take
> A tenderer meaning for thy sake,
> And all thou loved'st of earth and sky
> Seem sacred to thy memory!"

In 1843 the poems of Elizabeth Oakes-Smith appeared under his editorship; and he wisely supple-

Fay, Gould, Gilman, Halleck, Hale, Holmes, Hillhouse, Hoffman, Irving, Longfellow, Leggett, Lawrence, M'Lellan, Moore, Mitchell, Mellen, Norton, Neal, Percival, Peabody, Pierpont, Pinkney, Prentice, Pickering, Paulding, Rockwell, Sprague, Sutermeister, Sigourney, Simms, Sands, Smith, Street, Sargent, Tuckerman, Timrod, Woodworth, Wilcox, Willis, Wilde, Whittier, Wells."

mented his preface with a sketch of "Major Jack Downing" (the husband of the poetess), by John Neal, and an analysis of Mrs. Smith's genius and character, by Henry T. Tuckerman; thus bringing into general notice the literary proclivities and achievements of both writers, and winning for them immediate and appreciative regard. It was characteristic of him to do this, for he constantly sought, not only to encourage the efforts of laudable ambition, but to aid substantially in the recognition and the circulation of its fruits. Many a despondent author in those days was cheered and comforted by his generous sympathy; and, while still he recommended patience, he encouraged hope and would not entertain despair. In this same year he suffered his first domestic bereavement, in the death of his third child, a noble boy of five years. Playing with some companions on the pier near the South Ferry, at the foot of Atlantic Street, he accidentally fell into the river, and was drowned before succor could reach him.

> "Spring was unfolding like his own fresh life,
> When from the bosom of parental love,
> And boyhood's merry sports, an instant's strife
> Bore him all stainless to a home above." *

Out of the feeling engendered by this visitation of sorrow grew the little offering of sympathy called "The Mourner's Chaplet," a collection of American elegiac poems, carefully chosen for their consolatory spirit, published the following year. In the same year appeared

---
* "The Early Called," by Henry T. Tuckerman.

the first of his annuals—" The Wintergreen "—and it was probably about that time that he was also engaged in furnishing a large portion of the text for the quarto " North American Scenery, from Drawings by Whitefield." In 1846 he published " The Opal, a Pure Gift for the Holidays"; and its popularity induced the preparation of a second volume in 1847. "The Forest Legendary," a collection of metrical tales of the North American woods, appeared in 1848; and his gift-book, " The Floral Keepsake," in 1850. This completes the list of publications edited by Mr. Keese; and, although not a formidable one, it was much to have accomplished under pressure of business, which, far from ceasing with the day, demanded frequent nightly service. Viewed in no sense as original productions, the various works cited were, at least, so many evidences of good taste, literary discrimination, and a thoughtful consideration of the claims of genius; and there is something highly meritorious in the fact that all this painstaking labor was in obedience to an impulse to exalt our literature, and in dedication to the cause of refined culture. The education of the community always seemed to him a prime desideratum. He believed in the Baconian notion that knowledge is power; and it gave him the greatest satisfaction, at a later period of his life, to make public expression of his views in that regard, which he did in a lecture on " The Influence of Knowledge," delivered at the New York Tabernacle, in 1852.

The late Evert A. Duyckinck was of opinion that, had not my father been closely attached to the book business from his youth, he would probably have been an author. He certainly might have been a creator and worker in some department of literature; but I can not say that he was organized for systematic and sustained intellectual fulfillment. He would have been perspicacious as a critical essayist, admirable as a book-reviewer, expert and felicitous as a writer of *vers de société;* fertile in literary expedients, he might have made a successful journalist; but his mind was too alert and eager for the restraints of patient authorship. It was so much easier for him to talk than to write! He was a man of society; and what he said there, on the spur of the moment, drawn forth or suggested by the turns of conversation, was so much better and brighter than anything he could have produced by deliberation, that it is a question whether in subjection to imposed discipline he would not have lost in freshness and spontaneity. All things considered, I feel that his part was well taken, and I believe that no regret tinged his thought in any silent hour of retrospection.

He never, that I am aware of, made any attempt to collect his fugitive poems for publication. They were few in number and widely scattered. But, if all the jests, epigrams, and impromptu verses, that were his, and all the sonnets, valentines, dedicatory poems, etc., etc., written for friends, for years and years, should be printed, they would make a portly volume, and eloquently testify to the author's obliging disposition and good nature.

During most of the period mentioned above, our

family occupied a house on the north side of Atlantic Street, nearly opposite to where was once the eastern opening of the now-filled-in tunnel—which tunnel, by-the-way, was begun and finished while we lived there—and there some of the happiest years of my father's life were passed—years of prosperity and health; years fruitful in culture; years rich in genial companionship and intellectual communion; years golden in the memories they have left. It was there that he gathered around him a literary group, comprising names well known to a past generation, and the writings of many of whom still command respect and admiration.

The writer of these pages, like Halleck's "Fanny," was younger once than he is now; but he is not old enough to have belonged to that past in the sense that will permit him to paint that circle with the hues of memory. With the exception of Charles Fenno Hoffman and Henry Theodore Tuckerman, who were frequent and familiar visitors, recollection is dim and uncertain; and another pen must arrest and inform with light and color the shadowy figures of my retrospect. Happily for my readers, that pen is at my command, though the hand that wielded it so deftly lies pulseless in the grave.

In June, 1880, the late Henry Morford * wrote, and published in the magazine bearing his name, an appreciative and interesting sketch, in the course of which the identical group in question was drawn. I deem it especially good fortune to be thus enabled to complete my

---

* Henry Morford was born March 10, 1823, and died in 1881.

record of an important period; and, if any excuse were needed for introducing Mr. Morford's felicitous portraiture, it would be found in the remembrance of his warm attachment to my father, and in my gratitude for his expression of friendship.

A LITERARY GROUP
OF FORTY YEARS AGO.

[*Extracted from a sketch entitled "John Keese; his Intimates, etc." First published in "Morford's Magazine," June, 1880.*]

FORTY years have passed since the writer, then on the verge of manhood, came up to the city of New York, one Saturday evening, from his place of residence in the country, especially to remain over the Sunday, and to spend the evening of that day at John Keese's, on Atlantic Street, not far from Court Street, Brooklyn, almost exactly where, at that time (as the memory comes back to-day), ended the tunnel running up Atlantic Street from the South Ferry, for the use of the railroad to Jamaica.

What was the number of that house on Atlantic Street? Does the house still stand? Enough to say that the eye does not readily pick it out, if it exists: as a house, and for any purpose connected with this paper, it has ceased to be.

And yet this should not be so; for within the walls of that house, that evening and on many which followed, with and without the presence of the writer, was gathered a literary circle which has rarely been equaled in America in numbers, and which has scarcely ever had its superior in the quality of the persons composing it, except possibly now and again when so has gathered the literary force of the Middle States round Washington Irving in his golden days at Sunnyside, or when the culture of Boston and its clustering supplementary towns of Massachusetts has so gathered with Longfellow or Lowell or Holmes, in the days since England pronounced Boston the "intellectual center of the United States." If the old walls are still standing, they should have memories of the voices that forty years ago rang through them, in wit, pathos, and wisdom, only second to those clustering under the roof of banker-poet Sam Rogers, from the recollections of Thackeray, and Macaulay, and Hood, and Hook, and Barry Cornwall, and Lamb, and all that glorious circle, the very thought of which is bewildering to the commonplace mortal!

Is it possible to recall the names and the personalities of those who were present on that evening when the dazzled literary neophyte first set foot on that enchanted drawing-room carpet? No—possibly not: memory plays strange tricks, when there are many years in which to play them; and the best that can be done is to recall those who were to be found there, if not that special evening, at least on some of the other evenings rapidly following.

Shall we "reckon without the host," or even without the hostess? Assuredly, not so! Let John Keese, without whom those gatherings would never have been, have the first place of honor. A man of medium stature, thin and wiry in figure, with keen face, the nose markedly Roman and prominent, very heavy dark brows, almost meeting in the middle, and with a dark tuft at the root of the nose; eyes large, dark, and notably keen; mouth with a tendency to set itself a trifle tightly when in thought; full dark beard (the mustache not then worn, and to come later), full dark hair, with a dash of gray even then evident; thin, nervous, and expressive hands; and over all, and crowning the whole, a suggestion of quick, rapid, almost restless activity, as impossible to describe as to duplicate. Such was John Keese, of 1839–'40, as the memory comes back to-day: would the bright, active, restless, incorporeal self of the dear old friend recognize it, it may be wondered, if to-day, in another sphere, as thoroughly alive and all-observing as when so long ago it informed its energetic human tenement? This the host: how describe the hostess, who yet lives (thank God!), and upon whom the hand of Time has been laid more lightly than upon any other daughter of Eve in recollection? The very antipodes of her dark-haired, thin, and wiry husband. Blonde, blue-eyed, middle-statured, handsomely formed and featured, and youthful-looking enough for girlhood, though already the mother of three boys, one of whom, bright and sparkling Larry (Jonathan Lawrence), was to die, in service, in the ranks of the Seventh Regiment, in the opening days of the rebellion; the second, William Linn; and the third, little Willets, to perish by drowning, almost within sight of his home, before passing quite out of childhood.

Who next is entitled to place, of that circle certainly met on the first evening and very often after? Assuredly he of whom a leading English publication said, at very nearly the same period, that "his plume waved above the heads of all the literary men of America, a cubit clear"—Charles Fenno Hoffman. A man of tall figure, with broad shoulders and a general physique indicating that he had been originally intended for a man of robust habit, until accident and occupation had combined to thin him and, possibly, "fine" him a little. Bearing in appearance, gesture, and speech, evidence of the very good old blood to which he belonged; and a thorough gentleman at every point. A fine head, with dark-brown hair, quite decidedly inclined to wavy curl; whiskers of the same color and character quite surrounding the face, though with the lips and chin clean-shaven; a good and rather firm mouth; nose slightly low, though of fair length, and the reverse of aquiline; and pleasant eyes, well-browed, but always hidden behind the glasses made necessary by short-sight—such were, at that day, the features of the man who had written "Sparkling and Bright" (the finest Anacreontic ever penned on this side of the Atlantic), edited the "Knickerbocker" (at its commencement), afterward the "American Monthly" and the "New York Mirror," and published such notable volumes as "A Winter in the West," "Wild Scenes in the Forest and the Prairies," the novel of "Greyslaer" (followed afterward by "The Red Spur of Ramapo"), and much besides, holding high place in the world of American literature. Mr. Hoffman—though not all who met him were aware of the fact—had lost a leg in an accident, many years before, yet still remained the devotee of the field and the forest; and of the charm of his scholarly and dignified conversation only those can judge who heard him on such occasions as that under notice, at that crowning era of his life. Ten years later, when Zachary Taylor was President, and he held a government position at Washington, he was attacked by mental disease, lost his mind entirely (there were those who said that a woman's falsehood was the cause of the malady), and, through the thirty years that have elapsed since then, has lived the inmate of a Pennsylvania institution for the insane, forgetful of all that had been, his past fame, and perhaps even his identity.

Next, in that circle, one of the handsomest men of his day, and one of the most accomplished gentlemen and most irreproachable writers of any day—Henry Theodore Tuckerman. A figure of something more than medium height, with face slightly Roman in cast and Southern-European in suggestion; strong brows; pleasant dark eyes; close-cut, dark curling hair, and full beard and mustache, also dark and curling. Sweetly grave in manner, with flashes of absolute mischief in conversation. He had already, at that time, made the tour of Europe, producing his "Italian Sketch-Book" and "Isabel, or Sicily"; though the "Month in England," "Thoughts on the Poets," "Artist Life," "Characteristics of Literature," "Mental Portraits," etc., and that unrivaled series of essays, "The Optimist," were yet to follow at different periods of a life then yet very young. Perhaps no man of his age had more the faculty of winning blended respect and love; and few observers of character were so keen, as many of his after-publications well testified.

Perhaps the next place should be given to a lady—or at least to a lady and her husband. At that time Mr. and Mrs. Seba Smith were at something approaching the height of their fame, which had been a trifle meteoric, and was destined to be rather short-lived. Outside of the circle of personal acquaintance, not one in ten knew the real name of the short and undistinguished-looking man, with a certain Yankee shrewdness which made his conversation interesting while never deep or profound—"Major Jack Downing." The generation has now nearly all passed away who personally knew of and read at the time of their publication Mr. Seba Smith's one successful essay in life, "Major Jack Downing's Letters" from Washington and elsewhere, dealing with the capital, the President and his Cabinet and Congress, in the Yankee dialect, spiced with the gossip so easily picked up through the close observation of a Portland editor, and really forming, for some years, one of the current literary features of the period, until their collection into a volume in 1833, after which (as is the fate of many things written for an occasion) they very soon ceased to be remembered, and they and their writer were quickly overlooked if not forgotten. It was about that time that Mr. Smith was preparing for publication his most important work, "Powhatan, a Metrical Romance," which did not, however, take the country by storm, the best talent of the writer evidently lying in the epistolary walk before pursued. Before his death Mr. Smith also wrote many tales and sketches for the magazines, collected in 1855 or 1856, in " Down East "—and contributed to scientific education a work on the " New Elements of Geometry."

Of the rather handsome and undeniably attractive lady who was at that time the wife of " Major Jack Downing," much more might be said, as the lady filled a much broader place in literary history. Mrs. Smith had, personally, very handsome eyes; a high and full forehead, with waved light-brown hair swept down and sometimes hanging in ringlets on either side of the face ; a small and almost childish mouth, with a chin to correspond ; and a soft and pleasant voice which some of those who believed her addicted to coquetry regarded as a trifle affected. Willis considered that the Hon. Mrs. Norton had made, and worthily made, very much of her reputation by the exquisite title of one of her most popular poems, " The Undying One"; and he proved his belief by actually naming the lady after her heroine, in " Lady Jane":

> " All this time the ' Undying One ' was singing ;
> She ceased, and Jules felt every sound a pain,
> While that sweet cadence in his ear was ringing."

And it is not too much to aver that Mrs. Seba Smith won something like the same appreciation from the title of her best-known poem, "The Sinless Child." It first saw the light in the "Southern Literary Messenger," then (between forty and fifty years since) one of the leading literary publications of America, if not indeed the very first. Nearly at the time to which this paper refers, it gave title to "The Sinless Child, and other Poems," published in New York, where another volume of verse from the same pen had already preceded it. It had many fine lines, and was almost worthy the reputation acquired by it, as have been, before and after, a large part of the poetical labors of Mrs. Smith. It must have been at about this time that she gave to the world "The Roman Tribute," a five-act tragedy, and somewhat later another, local to New York colonial history, "Jacob Leisler." She also published, very little later, "The Western Captive," a novel; and a minor prose work, "The Salamander," attracted some attention, especially among the younger generation. The lady who at that time wore her brown curls of motherhood so coquettishly is still living, at what must be an advanced age; but she has long since ceased to be known, or spoken of by those meeting or remembering her, as "Mrs. Seba Smith." Long since, she became "Mrs. Elizabeth Oakes-Smith"—probably from some right to the name by blood, though not by birth, her maiden name having been Prince. Her sons, Appleton and Edward (both somewhat well known a quarter of a century since), went beyond the mother in her dilution of the name of Smith: they changed it altogether by linking the two halves together, and becoming "Oaksmith," not much to the content or honor, one would think, of the departed spirit of plain "Seba Smith" of the "Jack Downing Letters." But whatever the name, Captain Appleton Oaksmith, at least, made it notable in the detail of bravery: for the writer well remembers hearing an English commodore speak of him as "the devil and all, for pluck!" after his long and terrible fight of three days, with his ship and crew, against overwhelming odds, on the west coast of Africa.

There was another couple present on that first evening and not seldom after—Mr. and Mrs. Balmanno, whose names suggested their Scottish nationality, and who well sustained the national reputation by a broad heartiness, winning them many friends and not a few admirers. Both wrote—the wife (if memory does not fail) a little poetry and more of *belles-lettres* prose; and the husband, on many subjects connected with the history of his birth-land and the antiquities of Long Island. They were unexceptionable social companions, Mr. Balmanno especially; and years have not dimmed the recollection of his wealth of anecdote, embodying ancestral recollections of the days of Charles Edward Stuart, and reminiscences of all the great and notable of the previous century in the Land of the Thistle.

But here a fair, sweet presence rises—that of Frances Sargent Osgood, not a very frequent visitor, it is true, but occasionally to be found in that charmed circle, and when so found always delighting it. America has known no truer poetess than this lady, in all her years of nurture. No human face was ever more perfectly chiseled than hers—due regard having been had, meanwhile, to the fact that a woman, and not a statue, was being formed. That calm, pleasant face, those soft and kindly brown eyes, and that wealth of waved dark hair drawn low over her fair, white forehead, in the fashion of the time (since called the "Agnes Robertson"), won many a heart, the homage of which was kept by the always kindly and tender words flowing from the faultless lips seldom opened but to emit a sparkle. Mrs. Osgood returned to America, from London (where she had published a collection of poems with the modest title of "A Wreath of Wild Flowers from New England," and written a play called "The Happy Release," at the suggestion of James Sheridan Knowles), very soon after that first evening, and was thereafter, when she became a resident of New York, no infrequent sharer of those pleasant hospitalities. It was some years later that the fiend of disease laid his hand upon her, closing her honorable and popular career in 1850, and leaving in the minds of those who had known and loved her the belief that she had by no means done the best that was in her, even in such poems as "The Spirit of Poetry," "Labor is Rest," and the "Dear Little Truant."

And yet again, *place aux dames!* Oddly enough, while the mind of the writer can so well recall the pleasant word and the always welcome presence of Mrs. Emma C. Embury, no recollection remains of her looks. Let what she was and what she did atone for the lack of any personal description, in a paper not intended to be dependent on the recollections of others. Sometimes alone, and sometimes accompanied by her wealthy and socially distinguished husband, Mr. Daniel Embury, Mrs. Embury was often a member of that circle, bearing very modestly the honors of her varied publications, of which " Guido and other Poems " was the chief poetical exponent volume, while "The Blind Girl," "Pictures of Early Life," " Causes and Consequences," and other prose works in large number, in newspaper and other publications, gave token, and very little more, of what might have been had the authoress chosen to throw herself fully into a professional literary career.

What a strong, earnest face and what a Byronic head were those of William Gilmore Simms, who, once in a while, in some of his Northern visits, glanced in and out among the circle of visitors! That shaven face and the curly head above it were "all alive," as the phrase is —alive with the energy of the man who has been truly and properly called " the Walter Scott of the South "— equally excellent in prose and poetry; author of " Atalantis," one of the best imaginative poems that the country has even yet produced, and of so many historical and romantic prose works that nearly the same fatigue is involved in their mere naming, to be found in tracing the endless maze of Scott. There was something of John Wilson, of " Blackwood," too, in the man who was so thoroughly alive and earnest. At the time of which this paper treats, Mr. Simms was at about the glory of his early manhood—half-way between infancy and threescore and ten; and he had made the mark, some years before, of " Atalantis," and his first novel, " Martin Faber," and, very little before that time, of "Southern Passages and Pictures"—a most enjoyable medley. He was an indefatigable student, and equally indefatigable in the impartation of any item of knowledge in his possession, and the discussion of all the subjects relating to it; and those who remember him at that period can well understand the feeling with which Paul Hamilton Hayne wrote of him, when, two or three years ago, they inaugurated his monument at Charleston's Battery Park, and the sensations with which a whole people gathered around his grave, knowing and feeling that the South had lost one of the most distinguished of her men of letters, if not indeed the master of them all.

The next figure coming before the mind's eye, from the grouping of one of these notable evenings, belongs to a man who during many years created and endured as much excitement connected with the world of American literature as any other who could be named — Rufus Wilmot Griswold, ex-minister of the gospel, editor and literary worker in general, to whom the country really owed much, for a considerable period, and who was treated by that country more than a trifle irregularly before his death, as he has been, since that event, with a blending of neglect and captiousness. Mr. Griswold, at the time under notice (say at the earlier part of it), was about twenty-five years old, and had produced as yet very little work in the world of letters, though he had laid no mean foundation for doing so by quite extensive travels in Europe, by studying divinity, and becoming for a little time a preacher in the Baptist denomination. He was a man of rather small figure, a very intelligent face, with the eyes deep-set, good forehead showing an early inclination to the loss of front hair, sharp and trenchant nose, short, full beard and mustache (adopting the European fashion in advance of most other Americans), and a habit of holding down the head a trifle and looking keenly out from beneath the overhanging brows, not a little impressive when he was very much in earnest. Never profound, Mr. Griswold had a large fund of current intelligence, and was an exceptionally interesting talker, as possibly he had been a speaker of corresponding caliber. He was at that time connected with Horace Greeley's "New-Yorker," in an editorial capacity, as he either had already been, or was afterward to be (here memory fails again) with the "Brother Jonathan," "The New World," and other papers with literary tendencies. It was a little later that he became editor of "Graham's Magazine," doing more than any American had previously done to draw around a single publication the labors of the best thinkers of the country, and ably seconded, in doing so, by the far-seeing liberality of the publisher, Mr. George R. Graham, really the father of American magazines of the first class. Some years still later (probably about 1849 or 1850) he started "The International Monthly Magazine," with Stringer & Townsend as the publishers; and from 1842 till the time of his death, in 1856 or 1857, he was laboriously engaged in a series of compilations requiring that industry and that persistence of which he had so much, and demanding little of that absolute talent and that ripe scholarship, in both of which he was deficient. The number of his volumes became eventually much greater even than those of Gilmore Simms, though largely (as already said) compilations; and even to catalogue them would be no small task. Enough to say that principal among them in interest were " The Poets and Poetry of America," " Prose Writers of America," " Female Poets of America," " Washington and the Generals of the Revolution," " Napoleon and the Marshals of the Empire," " Curiosities of American Literature " (said to have been intended as a supplement to Isaac Disraeli's " Curiosities of [English] Literature "), " Republican Court " (suggesting or suggested by Huntington's picture of Washington's and Lady Washington's aristocratic and notable surroundings during the first presidency), etc. That Rufus Wilmot Griswold, the latter part of whose personal life was clouded by a most unfortunate marriage, and whose reputation has been worse pulled to pieces than that of any other man of the century, did great and meritorious services to our growing literature, and assisted in fostering many writers, who, without his encouragement, would hopelessly have laid down the pen, there is no question whatever; and it is something of a privilege, now that he has already been dead for nearly a quarter of a century, to call back, however dimly, his presence, and bear even this slight testimony to his labors.

And here a very different person, then at about the same age as Mr. Griswold, and one semi-deserting the bar for literature, as the other had quite deserted the pulpit for the same attraction. William H. C. Hosmer, a rather fine-looking and splendidly-voiced young man, with whom (though he is yet living and in the roll of native bards) the writer has never met since those early days. Mr. Hosmer was a native of Avon, in the Genesee Valley, son of Hon. George Hosmer, a well-known lawyer of Western New York, and of a mother who spoke some of the languages of the Indian tribes and made a study of their traditions. Naturally the young poet, who graduated at Geneva College, drifted into knowledge of and sympathy with the aborigines; and naturally his first poem (from the then yet unpublished pages of which, to see the light in 1864, he recited some of the scenes magnificently in those well-remembered evenings) was " Yonnondio ; a Legend of the Canadice." Mr. Hosmer's poetical works were published in 1854, largely spiced with Indian legends, in the handling of which he has probably never yet been excelled, but with an infinite variety in the compositions grouped around them, in scenes from European history, the Mexican War, etc.

A very tall young man joined in some of those memorable gatherings—a very tall young man, with a strong and not markedly handsome face, known as Richard Grant White. He talked well, and had a marked tendency to allude to the writings of one Shakespeare, of whom he appeared to be a " Scholar." He had also some very pronounced ideas connected with philology, giving promise that some day he might be heard from with reference to spellings, derivations, the morals of literature, etc. Very possibly he has really been so heard from: there has been for some years a man of the same name, connected with the New York Custom-House, if the memory of the writer is not at fault, who has written on such subjects, with an occasional run to English Stratford-on-Avon, and not a little pronounced familiarity with the works and belongings of the great dramatist. Can it possibly be that this is the very tall young man of forty years ago? and, if so, does he remember ever being at John Keese's, in the midst of such company as that of which some of the members have been already characterized?

Once in a while, a tall, slim-waisted, broad-shouldered young fellow of a little more than thirty, with curling, light-brown hair, trained a little in the direction of ringlets, an affectation of foreign beard, and somewhat more of other affectation than boded well for his eventual reputation, dropped in on the circle. He had also an addiction to colored coats and D'Orsay neckties, and was named Nat Willis—Nathaniel P. Willis, as he should have written the name; N. Parker Willis as he did write it generally. He had already, at this time, made the most extensive of his Old World travels, married Mary Leighton Stace, familiarized himself with English high life as few other Americans had ever done, and written his "Pencillings by the Way," awaking the admiring envy and the hostility of half the literary world. He had published a good deal of excellent poetry—some of it, especially "The Sacred Poems," never excelled before or since; and many of those who vilified him, and not a few of those who laughed at his affectations, recognized, then, and never afterward lost the recognition, that he was a man of true genius, with a "crank" or two promising decadence at the day when true excellence should properly be reached. Englishmen, then, and even earlier, knew him far better than they knew any other American; and it is betraying no secret to say that they disliked him not a little because he observed too closely. A rather affected but very charming talker, whose affectations were smoothed if not hidden by his evident talent and coveted wide experience—undeniably handsome, and knowing the fact far too well—really warm-hearted, though many mistook the cold polish for the heart it covered—a wise fool, who had and has many brothers on the earth, not all of them with the same redeeming qualities—such was Nat Willis, whom Father Prout was already lampooning as "Nick Willis," when the writer met him first in these reunions.

But this list must close, or be finished with only a few words, though the pleasant specters of those evenings rise very thickly. Thomas Buchanan Read, thin and earnest-faced, with somewhat long hair—poet and painter—then nearly at the same age as the writer, and with little of his life-work done. He had just removed to New York, had an opera in his mind, and talked very enthusiastically of it. "Boston," and the

"Lays and Ballads," were to come later, and then many years of celebrity as an artist at Philadelphia and in Italy, and the noble poetry of "The New Pastoral." Then—silence!——Colonel Thomas B. Thorpe—"Tom Owen, the Bee-hunter"—with his broad nose and face remindatory of Thackeray. Afterward to win laurels in the Mexican War, and in the volumes which grew out of it; to become a Brooklyn man, and die very recently, respected by all, at or past sixty.——"Charcoal Sketch" Joseph C. Neal, with his thin face and pleasant manner, and his conversation always suggesting the "Chalks on a Slab-Fence, by a Shingle-Splitter." To marry sweet Alice Bradley, a few years later; to leave her to do his unfinished work, and then to become Alice B. Haven.——The ardent, speaking face and concise, convincing language of Dr. Elisha Kent Kane, later to become one of the most distinguished of Arctic explorers and martyrs to science.——The almost baby face and long curls of Estelle Anna Lewis, newly a bride, and not yet accredited with her first volume of poems, which, and those following, marked her, as a sort of American Sappho the Lesbian.——And two more, Henry Inman, the painter, and his daughter.

Henry Inman was not only a noble artist, blending conscientious care with strong talent, and winning enviable reputation on both sides of the Atlantic, but he was a splendid-looking, dark-haired man, with the art of conversation very nearly reduced to a science. No amount of words could do justice to Mary Inman, once painted by Huntington as the most beautiful woman of her day, and well deserving the appellation. In face, word, and manner she was a born enchantress, with no little knowledge of the fact, and a tendency to flirtation (of the so-called harmless variety) which made many a young heart sore, and probably led away many a man, for a time, from his legitimate allegiance. What a star of beauty, grace, and vivacity she was, in those reunions! And how every man of the circle — especially if young and impressible—felt that here at last was the cynosure of a legitimate idolatry, and that he could "fill the bill" of that wayward, womanly demand! She was an exquisite vocalist, and a pianist of no ordinary power; and those who may chance to remember having heard her play and sing Hoffman's charming "Rosalie Clare" are not likely ever to forget the sensation. Witty beyond most of her sex, or indeed most of either sex, she was the chosen antagonist of John Keese in many of the wit-encounters of those notable reunions, and well bore her banner even in those perilous circumstances.

Such were the celebrities who from time to time gathered within the walls of the Atlantic Street house; and many a place, it may be said, has become historic through associations less distinguished. The house still stands; but no one nowadays, in passing it, dreams that its roof once sheltered so bright a circle of American *literati*. No neighboring memory recalls old scenes of joyous revelry—the toast, the song, the flash of wit, the flow of humor, the gay laughter; no reminiscence lives of the suggestive talk, the keen criticism, the tilt of intellect, the literary review, the winged idea, the birth of poem and story. Alas, the light of other days is faded—the light of the present day is a lantern over the doorway; and, where once resounded Hoffman's

> "Sparkling and bright in liquid light
> Does the wine our goblets gleam in,"

King Gambrinus waves a foaming "schooner" and invites the thirsty Teuton.

Often, in after-years, my father would dwell on that happy past, and interest us with recollections of many a famous evening, and of those who were actors in the scenes described. How few are living of all that bright array! Mrs. Oakesmith, Hosmer, Richard Grant White, Charles Fenno Hoffman, I believe, are all, and poor Hoffman's mental darkness is worse than death itself.* How well I remember him! He and Tuckerman, as before mentioned, were frequent and familiar visitors, and my brother and myself were often tutored by them in the recitation of their poems. Mr. Hoffman's "Sparkling and Bright" was my earliest committal to memory, and I can vividly recall my rather spasmodic interpretation of Mr. Tuckerman's "Apollo Belvedere." Then it was Mr. Hoffman's delight to equip us with shovel and tongs—which last article my father declared would do on a pinch—and

---

* Mr. Hoffman is in the asylum at Harrisburg, and remains the same as he has been for years. My last news of him is dated October 26, 1881, and then there was no change.

put us through a military drill, ending with a stern, peremptory "Dismiss!"—the obeying of which order was the one sole success of our performance. Mr. Hoffman was soldier, hunter, wit, poet, all in one, and, as I remember him, one of the most charming of men. He had a fund of stories of adventure, and drew toward him the young with a magic equal to that of the Piper of Hamelin. Mr. Tuckerman was more reserved in manner, but his warm heart was full of affectionate interest.

While in the enjoyment of the intercourse born of these memorable gatherings, the change occurred in Mr. Keese's business relations which, though it still claimed his allegiance to books, opened to him a new field and inaugurated a new career. For it was about this period that he severed his connection with the Collinses, and entered the co-partnership of Cooley, Keese & Hill, the business being the selling of books at auction, an enterprise destined to widely influence the circulation of literature, and in commercial magnitude to surpass all expectation.

The firm was at first located at what was then No. 157 Broadway; but the rapid growth of its affairs soon necessitated a removal to more spacious quarters; and the rooms at No. 191 Broadway, corner of Dey Street, were taken, the second floor serving as the sales-room and counting-house. It was there that the auctioneer, during an entertainment given to the trade in celebration of the new establishment, made the following announcement: "Gentlemen, we are casting our bread upon the waters, and expect to find it after many days—buttered!" There for years were held the semi-annual trade-sales, until the firm * moved to its final home in the splendid building at No. 377 Broadway, corner of White Street, where it continued to its dissolution in 1853 or 1854.

"Mr. Keese's accession to the firm"— wrote one who knew him at the time—"was undoubtedly invited by the other partners, from a knowledge of his immense acquaintance with both books and men, and probably from the additional fancy that his wit and readiness would be found of great advantage at the auctioneer's desk, which post he at once assumed, and where, within less than a year, he threw into the shade, from the exercise of his predominant qualities, any American auctioneer who had preceded him, as well as established a reputation somewhat closely approaching in prominence, and far excelling in the details of wit and enjoyability, that of George Robins in London."

The criticism is just. The celebrated George Robins was not, from all I can gather, remarkable as an auctioneer thoroughly well read in what came under his hammer, and endowed with a wit that amplified suggestion and illumined dull inanities; nor ready, on the instant, with felicitous word-play and repartee. His celebrity arose from his inimitable presentment,

---

* Cooley & Keese, Mr. Hill having retired previously.

as a whole, of the thing to be vended; his auction prospectus couched in terms so captivating that even hyperbole became charming, and what was impossible seemed easy and natural. Tom Hood sings of one—

> "The whole of whose birthright would not fetch,
> Though Robins himself *drew up the sketch*,
> The bid of 'a mess of pottage.'"

Everybody has heard the story of how Robins, after exhausting the language of praise in extolling a gentleman's park which was to come under his hammer, stated that he was bound, as an honest man, not to conceal the drawbacks to the property, which were "the litter made by the rose-leaves and the perpetual din of the nightingales." It was in such delicious pleasantries that Robins excelled; but it probably never would have occurred to him to reply to a purchaser, complaining that his book was damaged, "Damaged, you say? Yes, a little wet on the outside; but you'll find it dry enough within." Or, to a suspicious bidder, asking, "Is that binding calf?"—"Come up, my good sir, put your hand on it, and see if there is any fellow-feeling."

It is not, in the foregoing, specially designed to institute a comparison between the auctioneers. None is needed, could one be drawn. Each had his sphere and method; each was distinct in attributes and performance.

Certain it is, however, that Mr. Keese brought to the auctioneer's pulpit higher qualities than are usually found in that vocation. It seems fitting at this point to notice the tributes paid to his abilities by those who knew him, and who were well qualified to judge.

"I have the recollection of him"—wrote the late Evert A. Duyckinck—"as the wittiest book-auctioneer of his day in New York, and it may be said of any day, for there is no tradition of any predecessor of such powers, and he certainly left no successor in his peculiar vein. This may be said without disparagement to the intellectual cleverness of the Sabins,* Leavitts, and Merwins of the present day—for Keese was really an extraordinary man, in the humorous handling of books and an audience, enlivening a sales-room on the dullest of wet nights and under the most disadvantageous circumstances with the brilliancy of his wit. Few who attended his 'sales' did not carry away with them some recollection of his sparkling genius. It must have been a most impracticable book which did not in its subject, the name or associates of its author, furnish some opportunity for his pleasantry; and if these fell short he could eke out his merriment with some innocent play upon his audience."

The "peculiar vein" mentioned was an illuminating wit that played electrically upon every subject it touched, flashed light into nooks and corners, invested dull commonplaces with a hue of glory, and turned unmeaning or ambiguous title-pages into sudden and

---

* Mr. Duyckinck wrote in 1877. Mr. Joseph Sabin, the distinguished bibliographer, died in 1881.

felicitous revelations. Add to this a wide knowledge of books and authors, an exceptional memory, a keen perception of every vantage-ground, and, above all, a celerity in retort that was surprising—and you have an intellectual equipment rarely found in the possession of an auctioneer.

Selling a black-letter volume " Concerning the Apparel of Ministers," he supposed it referred probably to their " surplus ornaments "; and he assured his audience that the poems of the Rev. Mr. Logan were the "' Banks and Braes of Bonnie Doon '—at all events the brays."

"There was no quarter at the battle of Waterloo, my dear sir," he said to a bidder of twenty-five cents for a narrative of that conflict. " Really, this is too much pork for a shilling," was his pathetic remark at the sacrifice of a copy of Bacon's essays for twelve and a half cents. " Going — going — gentlemen — ten cents for Caroline Fry — why, it isn't the price of a stew!" (a jest prompted, perhaps, by a thought of the supper awaiting him at Dowling's, in Wall Street); and the same reflection probably suggested his interpretation of the title F. R. S. — " Fried, Roasted, and Stewed."

"Give the gentleman his book," he said, when an impatient buyer of Watts's hymns disturbed the sale by clamoring for delivery—" he wishes to learn and sing one of the hymns before he goes to bed to-night "; and, on knocking down another copy of the honored book, he ventured the parody:

"Blest is the man who shuns the place
Where other auctions be,
And has his money in his fist,
And buys his books of me!"

A volume by the Rev. Dr. Hawks was accompanied by the quiet observation, "A bird of pray, gentlemen." He knocked down Dagley's "Death's Doings" for seventy-five cents "to a decayed apothecary," with the consolatory comment of "smallest *favers* gratefully received"; and introduced a volume of impossible verse with, "This is a book" (glancing at the biographical sketch) "by a poor and pious girl—who wrote poor and pious poetry."

The following story of how the name of the author of "Woodman, spare that Tree" helped him to win over an audience and sell an impracticable book, went the rounds at the time. The occasion, I think, was when Colman's old Curiosity-Shop in Broadway was sold out.

"Here," said the auctioneer, presenting an antique-looking volume—"here, gentlemen, is a rare and valuable work — a collection of poems, odes, and all that kind of thing, addressed to the heroes and sages of the Revolution, and wedding to immortal verse the heroic events of that memorable epoch. These brilliant affairs emanated from the poet Armstrong, who in the early days of the republic contended with Joel Barlow and other choice geniuses for the laurel-wreath of poetry! A great poet, gentlemen! A wonderful man! How much shall I say for this copy of his works? Very scarce!"

A Mæcenas in the room, in an outburst of enthusiastic generosity, bid "twenty-five cents," and not a soul seemed inclined to advance upon it. "Only twenty-five cents! Such an offer is an insult to genius. Recollect, this Armstrong was one of the first American poets, celebrated in his day, though perhaps somewhat neglected in ours. He was a sort of Homer of the Revolution—the American Homer—think of that! How much for this rare copy of the American Homer?"

But the purchasers were deaf to the voice of the charmer. The "American Homer" could not extort another dime from the unpoetical assembly.

"Who knows," resumed the auctioneer, "but in after-years this man may be regarded by our posterity as the Virgil or Horace of the New World? Taste is capricious; but let it never be said that in the nineteenth century American citizens suffered the only volume of Armstrong's powerful and exquisite poems to go begging at twenty-five cents!"

But the names of Virgil and Horace awakened no more enthusiasm than that of Homer had done. The auctioneer looked round on the blank array of faces, and was about to knock down the book in despair, when another thought struck him, and he resolved on one more essay.

"Bear in mind," he said, "that this Armstrong was the General George P. Morris of his period. Like him, he was a hero and the laureate of heroes. He held a high military commission, and wrote impassioned, sentimental, and warlike songs on various themes. Like him, he combined in his own person the excellence of Pindar, Horace, and Tom Moore. Shall the works of the George P. Morris of the Revolution go for twenty-five cents? Forbid it patriotism! forbid it taste! forbid it refinement!"

The auctioneer "hit the right nail on the head" this time. This last appeal roused the enthusiasm of the bidders.

"Three shillings!" cried one.

"Fifty cents!" cried another.

For fifty cents it went; and to the fame of General Morris belonged the credit of extracting a quarter of a dollar from pockets that were closed against the several appeals of Homer, Virgil, and Horace.

In glancing over old papers, I am surprised to find so many tributes to my father's powers of entertainment. It would seem that in his day his qualities were deemed really phenomenal; and one of his admirers declared: "If John Keese should quit the auctioneer business, I should die of *ennui*. It would be a public calamity. He always looks to me like the ghost of Sheridan grown sick of Parliament, and just emigrated, and set up in the book-auction business in New York as a sort of practical joke on himself."

It was, then, a perfectly natural question for Mr. James Linen—in his poem of "The Auctioneer"—to ask:

"Who lives in old Gotham in comfort and ease,
And knows not the wit and wag, Auctioneer Keese?"

And the late Mr. James T. Fields, then of the firm of Ticknor & Fields, in his rapidly penned verses after one of the trade-sales, pleasantly sang:

"But all were gay, and every one
Before the feast agrees
That, when he wants for food or fun,
He'll shake a bunch of Keese."

To quote again from Mr. Duyckinck: "An auctioneer is bound to hold his own against all interlocutors. He is liable to all sorts of questioning and interruptions; but much of his success depends upon the maintenance of his powers in his seat of authority, his elevated pulpit. It is his business to control the audiences and their purses. To do this he must keep his company in good humor, and least of all suffer any intellectual discomfiture. Keese never lost this superiority. It was dangerous, unless particularly well armed, to enter into a contest with him. Any interruption of the business of the room was sure to be met by him, when no mischief was intended, in some gentle, playful way; but at the approach of anything like insolence the rebuke was severe."

A memorable instance of deserved punishment is related by Mr. Richard Grant White, in one of his notes to the American edition of "The Book-Hunter." Speaking of the auctioneer, Mr. White says: "He was courageous, too, as well as ready. At a sale of unusual interest, attention was attracted by the presence and the purchases of a notorious political bully, then in office, and since rewarded with a better place. The creature was as innocent of humane letters as of humanity of any other kind, and bought for some political satrap of higher culture, in whose service he was retained. He claimed a curious and valuable book which had been knocked down to the bid of another person. This was explained to him in vain, and he began at once to be abusive. It was then offered to put up the book again. But he refused consent to this arrangement, and began to threaten, exclaiming that he 'asked justice, and meant to have it.' 'Sir,' instantly replied Keese, in a distinct, low voice, as he fixed his steel gray eye upon the bully, who could have torn his slight little form to pieces, 'I know no man who deserves justice more than you do, and I heartily wish that you may get it.' The animal's hide was not proof against that dart. He turned livid with impotent rage, and slunk silently away."

The late Mr. Gowans was a familiar auditor at the sales, and bought extensively. He was very fond of calling the auctioneer out by putting questions concerning the book in hand, and the answers were always forthcoming. A work entitled "History of the Tatars" was offered. "Is not that Tartars?" asked Gowans. "No, their wives were the Tartars," was the immediate reply.

Some prayer-books were selling, and Gowans, as was his wont, interrupted the rapid vocalization with,

"Are they in English?" As quick as gunpowder came the answer: "Of course they are. Do you suppose a man is going to pray in Irish?"

An illustration of his readiness was when a parcel of fancy envelopes was passed up, to be sold in one lot. "How many are there?" was shouted from various parts of the room. "Oh, I don't know; too many to number—how much for the lot?" At last they were knocked down. "What name?" "Cowper!" "It shall be Cowper's 'Task' to count them," instantly exclaimed the auctioneer.

A joke much relished by the book-binding fraternity was his likening a ledger to Austria, because it was backed and cornered by Russia; and, when it was knocked down to a Mr. Owen Phalen, he paused at the name and said reflectively, "Don't know about selling to a man who is always Owen and Phalen."

He was felicitous in the application of a familiar quotation. Presiding over a consignment of furniture, which somehow had invaded the more legitimate business, he appealed over a coveted article to a hesitating housekeeper, "Going—going—'the woman who deliberates is lost'—gone!"

At one of such sales a table of curious design was sold to a bidder who left it to be called for. Some time elapsed, when a friend happening in admired the table and wished to buy it at private sale. He was told that it was sold to a party who thus far had proved himself one of the most un-com-for-table of men.

I remember, when a lot of Wade & Butcher's Sheffield razors was included in the catalogue, the auctioneer said that there was no limit to their sanguinary possibilities, for the buyer might "wade in blood and butcher all his friends." "Never mind, you'll have one volume less to read," he said to a bidder who found his set of books short; and when another wanted to know where the outside of his copy of Lamb was, the auctioneer conjectured that "somebody had fleeced it," adding consolingly, "But you can recover it, you know." A back-gammon board was put up, "to be sold on the square, and as perfect as any copy of Milton"—which comparison necessitated the explanation that there was "a pair o' dice lost"; and "Three Eras of a Woman's Life" elicited the running comment, "Wonderful woman—only three errors! How much?—thirty cents—only ten cents apiece—not very *xpensive errors, after all."

The feat of jotting down a report of my father's run of words at an evening sale was once accomplished by a short-hand writer; and I reproduce it here as a fair sample of the auctioneer's spirit when under the inspiration of the hammer.

"N'alf, n'alf, n'alf; three do I have? three, three; quarter, did you say? Never let me hear an Irishman cry quarter. N'alf, n'alf; knocked down to Maguire at three dollars and a half. Now, gentlemen, give me a bid for 'Hallam's Middle Ages', intended for gentlemen in the prime of life. Two dollars, two, two; an eighth, eighth, eighth; quarter, quarter, quarter—Moffat, at two dollars and a quarter. The next thing, gentlemen, is 'The Four Last Things, by Dr. Bates.' Fifty cents, fifty—'*What are they?*' Bid away, gentlemen, the book'll tell you exactly what they are: five eighths, five eighths; five and six. Chase has it, at five and six. Start, if you please, gentlemen, on 'Protestant Discussions, by Dr. Cummings,' an original D. D.—none of your modern fiddle-dee-dees: three quarters, quarters; seven eighths; do I have seven eighths?—yes, it is all complete; a perfect book, gentlemen; wants nothing but a reader. Dollar; dollar, n'eighth, n'eighth. Black has it, at a dollar and an eighth. Now, gentlemen, I offer you a superb 'Prayer Book,' Appletons' edition, best morocco, gilt all over, like the sinner; three quarters, three quarters, quarters, quarters—look at it, gentlemen. Here, sir, let me show it up to this goodly company; you've looked at it many a time with more care than profit: seven eighths; dollar; n'eighth; quarter, quarter — large print, gentlemen; good for those whose eyes are weak and whose faith is strong; remember your grandmothers, gentlemen—three eighths, three eighths. Brown has it, at one and three eighths. Now, gentlemen, I come to a line of splendid illustrated English books. Be so kind as to bid for 'Finden's Beauties of Moore,' cloth extra, full of superb illustrations, and I've how much bid for this? Start, if you please; go on. Two dollars; and a half, n'alf, n'alf; three, three; n'alf, n'alf; four, four, four. These are all English books, printed in England, bound in England, and sacrificed in America; and I have only four dollars for this superb book—quarter,

quarter, quarter, and this goes to Maguire, at four dollars and a quarter. 'The Gems of Beauty' is the next book, gentlemen. This is a glowing book, beautiful as Venus, and bound by Vulcan in his best days, red morocco, well read outside, gentlemen, and what do I hear for that? Fifty cents—horrible! Two dollars, by some gentleman whose feelings are outraged; quarter, quarter; half, shall I say? Cash has it, at two dollars and a half. Now, gentlemen, for the 'Philosophical Works of John Locke,' best edition, opened by John Keese; start, if you please—go on. Dollar; n'alf, n'alf; three quarters. *'Bound in muslin?'* Yes, sir; don't you respect the cloth? Seven eighths, seven eighths; two, two, two; quarter, quarter — brought three dollars the other day. *'No, it didn't!'* Well, one just like it did. Moffat takes it, at two dollars and a quarter. Now for a beautiful annual, gentlemen, 'The Ladies' Diadem,' splendid steel engravings, and no date, may be 1855, 6, 7, or 8. Can't tell; they publish them so much in advance nowadays. What do I hear? seventy-five, seventy-five; new book, published in England; dollar, dollar; eighth, do I hear? eighth; quarter; three eighths, three eighths—down. What's the name? whose bid is that? Well, just as you please; quarter, quarter—that's your bid, sir; 'gainst you, out there; three eighths—that's yours, sir; what's the name? *'I'll take it; you seem to be very anxious to sell it.'* No, sir, I'm not on the anxious-bench; those are the anxious-seats where you are. I take a decided stand on that; I face the whole congregation. Go on, if you please. The next book, 'Kirke White's Remains,' London edition, with splendid portrait, taken from some old daguerreotype; dollar, dollar, dollar, and down it goes. Who'll have it? Well, start it, gentlemen. What do I hear? seventy-five cents; seven eighths, seven eighths; dollar, by all the house; n'eighth, n'eighth. Cash has it, at a dollar and an eighth; horrible! I've been the high-priest of many a sacrifice. Now, gentlemen, who wants 'Ross's Last Expedition'? went to the poles, and, no doubt, voted twice. Start, if you please—go on; dollar, did you say? quarter, quarter, quarter; bidder here, half, half"—and so on through the catalogue.

It is no wonder that people flocked to the evening sales; and I have heard many say that to go there was as good as a play; so that the late William E. Burton, to whom in after-years my father became warmly attached, whose theatre was then in Chambers Street, regarded the auction-room of Cooley & Keese as no contemptible rival. And here I am reminded of an experience related by the famous comedian, which, although a tale of his own crushing discomfiture, was told with great relish. The story is new, and is really too good to be lost.

It annoyed Burton very much when, in the tag end of the play, certain of the audience began the bustle of departure, and he determined to embrace the first opportunity to administer a public rebuke. He had not long to wait. One evening, toward the close of the piece, the characters standing in order for the epilogue, an auditor arose in the gallery-front and began to button up his coat. The comedian left his place and stepped to the foot-lights. "Excuse me, sir, but the play is not finished, and you disturb the audience. Have the goodness to sit down." The stranger, without pausing in his preparation, promptly replied: "Can't help it. I've listened to your infernal trash long enough, and now I'm going." "And what did you say, Burton?" exclaimed the late Henry Placide, who was one of the amused group. "Harry," said Burton, with an air of complete humiliation, "I couldn't say a —— word!" My father was quite right in thinking that the actor received on that occasion emphatically a curtain-lecture.

A few words more with regard to Mr. Keese's value as an auctioneer. A man of his knowledge and ability was something entirely new in that capacity, and his qualities could not fail to make an impression upon contemporary publishers. The success which attended the semi-annual trade-sales was largely due to his comprehensive management of their important details, and his zealous attention to the interests of all concerned. I may be pardoned for quoting from an editorial article in a New York paper of the period, under the heading "Our City Trade-Sales," the following generous tribute. After remarking on the extent of a late sale (the largest that had taken place at the time), the article proceeds: "We can not, however, refrain from a word or two on this subject with reference to the minor causes which help to produce such extensive business transactions. It is well known that in a trade-sale there is something more than capital required to carry on the sale. Money, it is true, as the old saying is, begets money: but, never to such extent as when it is aided and directed by the capital of the mind. This is to be clearly seen in the case of the late trade-sale. A large amount of money capital was undoubtedly invested— no house, perhaps, is ready to invest a larger in the same range of business; but, to the unceasing, indefatigable, and persevering efforts of the auctioneer himself, Mr. John Keese, is to be attributed a main cause of so extensive a sale having taken place. With reference to Mr. Keese personally we have no interest: we know him only from report, and that report, emanating from men whose dealings at the trade-sales have been constant, is strong concerning him. It may seem, indeed, a matter of indifference who may take upon himself to arrange a sale and offer books to public competition. But in truth it is not so. It is of great importance to all concerned that the man, who at such times places himself in the rostrum of the auctioneer, should himself be well acquainted with all the minutiæ of the business, and should be perfectly familiar with the books, both externally and internally, that pass through his hands; and, not only that, but should also be possessed of that particular tact and ability which enable him to keep his audience constantly with him in fresh and cheerful company. In Mr. Keese we have in our visits to these sales noticed these qualifications particularly. We have, moreover, been at times delightfully surprised on witnessing the natural and easy manner with which he carried on the sale without the slightest forcing for effect, and the light and life with which he managed to disperse its monotonous character, diffusing cheerfulness over all his hearers. There were flashes of brilliant wit and sentiment ever emanating from him; and the occasional lively repartee tended to produce in the room that good humor and feeling so essential, while it drew upon him hearty marks of applause. Then, again, his sound acquaintance with every branch of literary work was evident; his knowledge of the value of a book, its worth intrinsically, and its marketable price in the store; his familiarity with the writings of the Eastern sages and classic Greeks, the Latin orators, and the learned of modern times; his apt quotations and remarks concerning living authors—all of which tended to convince us that superiority of intellect, of education and experience, preeminently adapted Mr. Keese for the position he had assumed; and it was also clear that he possessed that practical knowledge of business, that promptitude and activity of habit, which are essential to all who seek success; and we have no hesitation in saying that he assuredly deserves it. His visits to the various cities of the Union, in connection with the trade-sales, have caused him to be well known in many places, and everywhere to be esteemed; and we have thought it right to allude thus personally to him, because we always like to see the energy and perseverance of a fellow-citizen properly appreciated and understood. That this is so with reference to Mr. Keese the trade in the late sale have undoubtedly admitted. Confidence in his name was felt by every buyer; and the same feeling existed in the minds of all those gentlemen who semi-annually offer their books to public sale through him and the well-known house with which he is connected. Most cordially do we wish him a continuance of that success which his persevering efforts are so much entitled to."

I can not repress an emotion of pride while penning the foregoing, and my thanks are recorded here to the unknown writer for so feeling and so appreciative a tribute.

The out-of-town visits referred to were always a source of pleasure to Mr. Keese, for, while they extended his business connections, they also brought him into familiar intercourse with prominent publishers and men of letters, and many valued friendships grew out of the association. This was particularly the case in Boston and Philadelphia. In the former city he was introduced to Longfellow, Holmes, and others of the Boston *literati*. We have in our possession an elegant edition of Longfellow's ballads, a gift from the poet himself, containing on the fly-leaf the sixth verse of " The Psalm of Life," written there by the revered author's own hand. What a treasure the volume has now become I need not say!

The kind offices of the late James T. Fields were of great value to my father in those days, and many an introduction to men of note he owed to Mr. Fields's friendly interest. I have always fancied that much intellectual sympathy existed between the two. They were about the same age; their qualities of mind were not unlike;

they were equally interested in letters, and full of enthusiasm respecting their favorite authors and the literary guild generally. The aspirations of Mr. Fields were more than answered. It fell to his lot to enjoy the acquaintance, if not the friendship, of more literary people of eminence than any American of his time; and he died full of years, beloved and lamented; but not before having given to the reading public a record of delightful memories.*

Philadelphia, though by no means the haunt of authors as compared with Boston, was a pleasant place to visit, and Mr. Keese's relations with the publishers there were always cordial. Undoubtedly his name is still remembered by many of the old houses. I am reminded of a ludicrous incident he was witness of on one of his visits, which, on account of its professional flavor, amused him greatly. Strolling out at evening, he came to a street where he found a little auction-store in full blast, and with fraternal interest dropped in, to see what was going on. A fiddle was "going" in the hands of the auctioneer: "How much for this very fine fiddle?—how much?—dollar—going—and a half—shall I have three-quarters?—dollar and a half—going—gone! Now, gentlemen, we'll sell the bow!" "Why, I thought I bought the bow with the fiddle," exclaimed the amazed bidder. "From the country, I presume, my friend," replied the auctioneer, with bland politeness; and the bow, I believe, was knocked down as a separate lot. He used to tell this story with great glee; and it is quite probable that

---

* "Yesterdays with Authors."

had a fiddle and bow ever been included in an invoice to Cooley & Keese, he would have found it hard to resist the temptation to experiment upon his audience with the tactics of his Philadelphia brother.

Mention has been made of Mr. Burton, the famous comedian. He was also a Shakespearean scholar, a man of letters to some extent, a lover of books, and the possessor of one of the finest private libraries in the country. Naturally, catalogues of all sales of interest and value were sent to him, and my father kept him informed with respect to the character and desirability of collections to come under his hammer—besides, as the demands of his profession would not permit Mr. Burton to attend in person, managing his bids and buying for him at the sales. An acquaintance easily grew from this connection, and a friendship later. One of Mr. Burton's reciprocal acts of kindness was to place our family on the free list of his theatre, and the many hours of delight born of that enviable privilege are still in the keeping of memory. Those were the days of *Captain Cuttle*, *Paul Pry*, *Aminadab Sleek*, *Timothy Toodle*, *Sir Toby Belch*, *Autolycus*, and the rest; the days of Placide, Blake, Brougham, Lester, George Barrett, T. B. Johnson, Mrs. Hughes, Mary Taylor, and a host of others; and the present writer has recorded in another form his recollections of nights at the Chambers Street Theatre.

The design of forming an "American Shakespearean Club" was conceived at this time, and a complimentary dinner was given to Mr. Burton, by some friends and admirers, on the 23d of April, 1852, when an organization was effected. Mr. Robert Balmanno, already mentioned in the literary group sketched by Mr. Morford, acted as secretary on the occasion, and an account of the festivity was written by him and published in the "New York Evening Mirror" of April 26th. As Mr. Keese warmly espoused the cause, and was chairman of the meeting, I quote a portion of Mr. Balmanno's report:

"In the course of the evening, Mr. Burton exhibited to the company a most gorgeous Shakespearean silver cup, of bounteous capacity, and of the most classic shape and proportions, superbly chased with some of the most prominent of Shakespeare's characters, executed from a drawing made by the celebrated Stothard. This contained another cup fashioned from the wood of the far-famed mulberry-tree which was planted by Shakespeare's own hand in his garden at Stratford-on-Avon—and the well-known words of the song will apply, when Garrick held up *his* cup at the Stratford jubilee:

"'Behold this fair goblet;
'Twas carved from the tree
Which, O my dear Shakespeare,
Was planted by thee!'"

After an admirable dinner, the most important business of the evening was entered into: namely, the formation of an American Shakespearean Club; and an admirable letter from Washington Irving was read, with other letters and papers. Mr. Irving, it seems, had been invited to fill the office of president; but he had declined, and Mr. Burton was proposed and unanimously elected.

In rising to propose a toast in honor of the day, Mr. Keese said: "Gentlemen, we are met this evening in a social and informal manner, to do honor to the nativity of the highest literary genius the world has ever known. It would be sheer presumption in one to whom your partial kindness has dictated his present position, to descant for a moment upon the genius whose myriad-mind has been illustrated by the greatest men that have come after him; and in the presence of the truest living exemplifier of one department of his characters, and the severe and appreciating students of his works. What could I say, that all of you have not better thought, and much better said, before? It is a great day that we celebrate—the greatest in the intellectual calendar of time. Is it not one that will ever be commemorated with enthusiasm? Yes! while there are stars in heaven, or an Anglo-Saxon upon earth! Gentlemen, I give you— The day we celebrate: it will ever be a *celebrated* day."

The remarks of the chair, wrote Mr. Balmanno, introducing the toast complimentary to Mr. Burton, were in Mr. Keese's happiest vein. He claimed for him a combination of the versatile characteristics of four renowned English comedians—Emery, Fawcett, Munden, and Liston—and most felicitously remarked, that could his great master, Shakespeare, have witnessed Mr. Burton's inimitable delineation of *Polonius*, *Touchstone*, and *Sir Toby Belch*—his incomparable personation of *Autolycus* in the "Winter's Tale," and even that of the weird sisters in "Macbeth"—he would have hugged him to his heart with the same burst of feeling which has been transferred from the lips of Shakespeare to the tomb of one of his choicest comrades, and truly exclaimed—

"O rare Bill Burton!"

Here, said the chronicler, Mr. Burton rose; no longer the irresistible magician who sets in movement every mirthful emotion of the heart; but grave, impressive, and dignified; and in a brief but most eloquent speech expressed as well in manner as in words how deeply he felt the friendly homage by which he was surrounded.

The association so auspiciously begun was destined to be short-lived. I have no record or recollection of any of its subsequent meetings; and the promise that it gave of establishing in New York an institution devoted to noble uses, and worthy of its great name, was, unhappily, not fulfilled.

Some time after the dinner above described, Mr. Burton gave a "Mulberry Feast" in honor of Shakespeare, at his residence at Glen Cove, Long Island. The late Lewis Gaylord Clark, in describing the occasion, in his "Editor's Table" in the "Knickerbocker," tells the following story, in which Mr. Keese appears:

"At this festivity the late Mr. Balmanno, the kindly devotee to the great dramatist and the whole genial world of literature and art, unwrapped from many foldings of tissue-paper a piece of bark, taken by himself, as he asserted, from Herne's oak in Windsor Forest. 'You took this from the trunk of the old oak itself, did you, Mr. Balmanno?' asked Keese. 'I did,' was the response. 'Ah!' was the reply of his questioner, eying the relic with affectionate admiration, but thoughtfully, after a slight pause—'isn't it barely possible, Mr. Balmanno, that you may have been *barking up the wrong tree?*'"

The following lines are taken from a local poem written for a literary society at the time when Burton's Theatre was deservedly the most popular place of amusement in the city:

> "The drama flourishes, and one thing's certain,
>   Wealth, taste, and beauty throng to laugh at Burton.
> There they behold great Shakespeare's finest scholar,
> A poet and a wit, for half a dollar;
> There Shakespeare, Sheridan, and Colman, meet,
> And you must early go to get a seat.
> Rare son of Momus, may your shadow ne'er be less,
> And we not die from laughing to excess!"

Nor did he forget the renowned importer of Jumbo:

> "The Bearded Lady, with her whiskers dark,
> Is seen each day at Barnum's, near the Park.
> Barnum exhibits, with his usual taste,
> His only humbug that is not barefaced!"

It may not be out of place to give here a single specimen of a light kind of verse-writing; the only one out of many that chance has preserved. The lines are addressed

TO A DAUGHTER OF NEW ENGLAND,

On the receipt of a Pumpkin-Pie on Thanksgiving-Day.

Thanks, lady, thanks!—thy hand well skilled
  To touch with fairy fingers
The harpsichord with music filled,
  As o'er it beauty lingers—

Didst thou descend where plate and platter
  In goodly order stand,
And form for me this pretty batter,
  This gift from Yankee land?

Oh, were I blest with wit and taste
  Well seasoned as thy pie,
I would in numbers *puff* thy *paste*,
  Nor make a *tart* reply.

Thou modest pumpkin! gentle hands
  Did pluck thee from the vine,
And made thee pride of Eastern lands
  Whene'er their children dine.

And though thou wert of modest birth,
  Nay, groveled in the dirt,
Yet all New England knows thy worth,
  And owns thy rich *dessert!*

And Pilgrim daughters on this isle,
  Where *squashes* most abound,
Will greet thy presence with a smile,
  When Thanksgiving rolls around.

Then, lady, will my prayers ascend
  For richest gifts on thee;
And Heaven will bless the gentle friend
  Who shares her *crust* with me.

And though I fear my own desert
  Will ne'er awarded be,
My flattered fancy must revert
  To one sweet *puff* from thee.

And should I run the race of fame,
  I'll feel with joy elate
That no dishonor clouds his name
  Who's *won a lady's plate!*

A passing allusion to Mr. Burton's library has been made in these pages; but a more extended reference to it can not fail, I think, to interest my readers. Let me recall the evening when it was my privilege to stand within those walls, sacred to the glorious and immortal in literature, and adorned with inestimable treasures of art. It was an evening when Mr. Burton had gathered about him a band of friends, and the writer accompanied his father, who was one of that chosen circle. With what trembling awe I found myself in the presence of the elder Wallack, his son, Mr. Lester, Henry Placide, George Barrett, Dion Boucicault, and the great comedian himself! That indefinable sensation—which I suppose every youth experiences when finding himself in the company of actors off the stage—possessed me as I furtively gazed upon those faces I had never before seen this side of the foot-lights; and as I looked at Mr. Wallack I thought of *Erasmus Bookworm* and *Dick Dashall;* the agreeable presence of Mr. Lester evoked the images of *Percy Ardent* and *Harry Dornton;* I expected to hear the voice of *Colonel Hardy* when Mr. Placide spoke; in the tall person of Mr. Barrett I saw the boastful bearing of *Bobadil;* and in the host himself was reflected an entire gallery. But, really, there was nothing of the kind. They were so many gentlemen gathered beneath Mr. Burton's roof, enjoying his hospitality, and acting simply their natural parts. The profession was dismissed. Like a man's business, it was over for the day. Yet, at supper, the qualities that so often shone on the mimic scene came into play, and lent to conversation vivacious flow and sparkle. "The flash of wit—the bright intelligence"—gleamed about the board, everywhere finding an answering spirit, and prolific in entertaining contribution. A topic launched by Mr. Barrett, Mr. Wallack would gayly seize and build upon; Mr. Lester would then playfully and characteristically paraphrase it; Mr. Placide would in turn secure it and augment it felicitously—and so on; until finally it was received by Mr. Burton, to be amplified with infinite relish.

But a greater treat was in store. Supper ended, we were invited to the library.

This structure was a building by itself, and was connected with the residence by a conservatory gallery, through which the company passed. The principal library-room was on the upper floor, with lofty, ornamented ceiling, in the center of which rose a dome skylight of stained glass. We saw the bookcases, upward of nine feet high, lining the sides of the room, in whose oaken recesses reposed over sixteen thousand volumes! Masterpieces of painting hung in the space between the cases and the ceiling, and wherever our eyes turned they were held by some object of artistic design, historic interest, or haunting beauty. Mailed effigies in niche and compartment embalmed the stern glory of the middle ages; the divine wonder in the eyes of Mary in "The Nativity" looked forth from the canvas of Murillo; and the spirit of Shakespeare held sceptered sway, breathing from sculptured image, bust, and cenotaph, and many a priceless relic. We gazed upon an equestrian picture of Queen Victoria—the Queen painted by Count d'Orsay, the horse by Landseer—which picture now adorns the wall of the Conservative Club in London. The Murillo, I may note, became the property of the Peruvian Minister to England, who considered it of fabulous value.

In a prominent niche stood a full-length statue of Shakespeare, executed by Thom, the Scotch sculptor; and on another side of the library, on a bracket of the Elizabethan age, was placed the Stratford bust—bracket and bust both obtained by Mr. Burton at the sale of the effects of the celebrated antiquary, Mr. Cottingham, and no other copy of them, it was said, existed. There was a curious cup, found in Shakespeare's garden; a beautifully carved tea-caddy, made from the wood of Shakespeare's mulberry-tree, once the property of Garrick; a small statue of Shakespeare in china, remarkable for being the first specimen of that ware executed at Chelsea in England, and historic, like the tea-caddy, in that it also was formerly Garrick's; two drinking-cups with silver rims, said to be "made of the wood of a crab-tree under which Shakespeare slept during his celebrated frolic, formerly in the possession of Betterton." Outside the library, in a place prepared for it, stood the statue of Shakespeare in wood, a relic of the old Park Theatre. Among other relics not pertaining to Shakespeare, but of equal historic interest, were the gold watch presented by Napoleon to Talma, the tragedian, with an interior inscription; Washington's own repeating watch; and many other interesting mementos.

It is not my intention, even were it possible, to attempt any description of the many rare and valuable books that were embraced in Mr. Burton's superb collection. Too young to have any comprehension whatever of those thousands of volumes of precious literature, I can only record my condition of simple wonderment as I stood and gazed around me. That matchless library was sold at auction after the owner's death, and suffered, I believe, general dispersion. I know, however, that every department of literature, exclusive of the Shakespearean collection, was represented, and comprised works of acknowledged bibliographical eminence, many being unique in importance and value.*

---

* A detailed description of Mr. Burton's library will be found in an account of "Private Libraries in New York," by James Wynne, M. D., published by E. French, New York, 1860.

I have often wondered why my father, with his many opportunities, never amassed a library. Perhaps it was owing to the fact that his business was books, and, being constantly in the midst of them, there was no incitement to pursuit and possession. A collection of books at home might have seemed to him, indeed, something like a transplantation of his business. But, at all events, he gave no sign of a collector's itching palm, nor of anything that betokened a leaning toward bibliomania. He would bring books home to read and to show us, and would then take them away; they were not so many adding prizes to groaning shelves. Not but that all our literary needs were more than supplied; but he did not share Henry Ward Beecher's feeling that there is no pleasure so great as that of buying a book you can not afford to pay for. He could not say with *Prospero*, "My library was dukedom large enough."

The dissolution of the firm of Cooley & Keese in 1854, as previously stated, compelled my father to seek a new position, and he obtained the appointment of Appraiser of Books in the New York Custom-House, a post he was well qualified to fill. So long as his health permitted, he still occupied the auctioneer's pulpit at the evening sales of the firm's successors; but the exertion was always followed by sore aggravation of his bronchial trouble, and at length it became evident that his selling-days were over. He confined himself then to his duties as appraiser, and felt hopeful that with care his season of usefulness might be prolonged. But it was not to be. His voice rapidly failed, until it fell to almost a whisper. Yet his bright spirit still watched the citadel. In so dark an hour, Chief-Justice Daly, meeting him at his labor, inquired respecting his health. "Failing, failing—in a place where everything is *invoiced* except myself."

He grew weaker and weaker, and finally was unable to leave his room. In the afternoon of May 30, 1856, his brother brought from the Custom-House a document requiring his signature, and he wrote his name with a firm hand. A few hours afterward he was no more. A sudden hæmorrhage was the immediate cause of death; and with the shadows of evening came the deeper shadow of bereavement.

So passed away a man who thirty years ago enjoyed a reputation almost unique in the city that gave him birth. With respect to natural gifts and certain predominating qualities, it seems to have been generally acknowledged that no successor in the auction-room has suggested a comparison. His career was marked by activity and enterprise, and in the performance of his duties he exhibited zeal, method, and comprehension. His physical endurance was remarkable, and he shrank from no labor, however fatiguing or incessant. It was no unusual thing, during the trade-sales, to see him go on selling day after day, as fresh and sparkling as if he had just come on the stand. An endeavor to depict him in the scenes of his busy life has been made in the preceding pages, and I trust not wholly in vain. Allusion has been made to his conversational and entertaining powers, and his name may be recalled by readers of this memoir who remember him in the social circle. It remains to be said that he was kind and loving in his family relations, and that his home was everything to him. He was generous to a fault, and ever ready to respond to friendship's call. His motto might be given in the words of Shakespeare:

> "I count myself in nothing else so happy,
> As in a soul remembering my good friends."

INDEX.

Allston, Washington, 33, note.
"American Shakespearean Club," 79.
"Ancient Mariner, The," 15, note.
"Attic Club, The," 12, note.
"Auctioneer, The," quotation from, 66.

Balmanno, Mr. and Mrs., sketch of, 47.
Balmanno, Robert, 80, 81, 82, 83.
Barker, J. N., 33, note.
Barlow, Joel, 64.
Barrett, George, 79, 85, 86.
Beecher, Henry W., 89.
Biddle, Nicholas, 24.
Bigelow, John, 12, note.
Bird, R. M., 33, note.
Blake, William E., 79.
Boucicault, Dion, 85.
Bradley, Alice, 56.
Brooks, J. G., 33, note.
Brougham, John, 79.
Bryant, William Cullen, 20, 31, 33, note.
Burr, S. J., 33, note.
Burton, William E., 30; story of, 73; mention, 79, 80, 81, 82, 85, 86, 87, 88.
Burton's Theatre, 83.
Butler, George B., 12, note.

Canfield, Rev. Dr., 10.
Chapman, J. G., 21.
Cheever, George B., 31.
Choate, Rufus, oration of, 13.
"Christabel," 15, note.
Cincinnati, Society of the, 7.
Clark, Lewis G., 21, 24, 82.
Clark, Willis G., 33, note.
Clarke, Dr. Alonzo, 12, note.

Collins & Hannay, 8.
Collins, Keese & Co., 9, 20.
Colman, Samuel, 33, note.
"Column Club, The," account of, 11, note.
Cooley, James E., 9.
Cooley & Keese, 9, 60, 73, 79.
Cooley, Keese & Hill, 9, 59.
Cooper, J. Fenimore, 21, 24.
Cornwall, Barry, 40.
Cutter, W., 33, note.

Dana, R. H., 33, note.
Daponte, C. E., 33, note.
Davidson, L. M., 33, note.
Davis, Matthew L., 22, 23.
Dawes, R., 33, note.
Dearborn, George, 20.
Dewey, Rev. Orville, 20.
Dinnies, A. P., 33, note.
Doane, G. W., 33, note.
Drake, J. Rodman, 22, 33, note.
Duyckinck, Evert A., preface, 36, 62, 67.

"Early Called, The," 35, note.
Ellet, E. F., 33, note.
Embury, Daniel, 49.
Embury, Emma C., 33, note; sketch of, 48.
Emery, John, 81.
Evarts, William M., 12, note.
Everett, Edward, 24, 33, note.

Father Prout (Francis Mahony), 55.
Fawcett, John, 81.
Fay, Theodore S., 34, note.
Felt, David, 20.
Fields, James T., 30; verse by, 67; mention, 77, 78.

INDEX.

Fish, Hamilton, 12, note.
" Floral Keepsake, The," 36.
" Forest Legendary, The," 36.
Forney, John W., 17.
Forrest, Edwin, recitation by, **17**.
Francis, John W., 21, 23, 24.

Gallatin, Albert, **20**.
Gilman, Caroline, 34, note.
Godwin, Parke, 12, note.
Gould, H. F., 34, note.
Gourlie, John, 12, note.
Gowans, William, 68.
Gray, Harrison, 21, 22.
Griswold, Rufus W., sketch of, **50–52**.

Hale, Sarah J., 34, note.
Halleck, Fitz-Greene, **20, 21, 24, 34**, note, 38.
Harper, Fletcher, 20, 25.
Harper, James, 21, 22 ; speech of, 23.
" Harper's Magazine," **30**, note.
Haven, Alice B., 56.
Hayne, Paul H., 50.
Hill, Horatio, 9.
Hillhouse, J. A., 34, note.
Hoffman, Charles Fenno, 34, note, 38 ; sketch of, 42, 43 ; mention, 57, 58, note, 59.
Hoffman, George H., **12, note.**
Holmes, Oliver W., 34, **note, 40, 77**.
Hone, Philip, **21, 23**.
Hood, Thomas, 40, **61**.
Hook, Theodore E., 40.
Hooper, **Lucy**, " Poetical **Remains** " of, 33.
Hosmer, William H. C., sketch of, 53, **58**.
Hughes, Mrs., 79.
Huntington, Daniel, 52, 56.
Hutton, Laurence, story told by, **28**.

" **Idiot Boy**, The," poem, 16–20.
" Influence of Knowledge, The " (lecture), 36.
Inman, Henry, 21 ; sketch of, **56**.
Inman, Mary, sketch of, 56.
Irving, Washington, 20, 21, 23, **24**, 34, note, **40**, 80.

Johnston, T. B., **79**.

Kane, Elisha Kent, **56**.

Kean, Edmund, 27, 28.
Keese, Edmund Willets, 10.
Keese, John (grandfather of subject), 7.
Keese, John, preface, **birth, and parentage**, 7.
  his grandfathers, 7.
  education for the ministry, **8**.
  beginning his business **career**, 8, 9.
  marriage and family, 9.
  self-cultivation, **10, 11**.
  joins " The Column Club," **11**.
  love of **oratory**, Brougham, Choate, etc., **13**.
  Dr. Nott's addresses, **14**.
  Kossuth's speeches, **15**.
  poetical recitation, 15.
  improvisation and reading, 15, note.
  " The Prisoner of Chillon," **16**.
  " The Idiot Boy " ; Forney and Forrest, 16–20.
  Booksellers' dinner, speech thereat, 20–25, *et seq.*
  a genuine Gothamite, **26**.
  extract from local poem, **26**, 27.
  passion for the drama ; imitations of actors, **27**.
  auction-room story, 28.
  private theatricals ; " The Rivals," **29, 30**, *et seq.*
  editorship ; " The Poets of America," etc., etc., 31–36, *et seq.*
  " The Influence of Knowledge " (lecture), **36**.
  his literary **capabilities** ; productions, 37.
  residence in Atlantic Street, 38.
  A literary group, 39–57.
  pen-portrait of, **41**, *et seq.*
  fate of Atlantic-Street house, 57, *et seq.*
  becomes auctioneer, 59.
  qualities as auctioneer, 60–63.
  wit of the auction-room, **63–73**.
  value as an auctioneer, 74.
  encomium in New York paper, **74–77**.
  out-of-town visits, 77, *et seq.*
  story of Philadelphia auctioneer, 78.
  acquaintance with W. E. Burton, 79.

INDEX.

Keese, John, presides at meeting of Shakespeare Club, 80.
  speeches thereat, 81, 82.
  story of, at " Mulberry Feast," 82, 83.
  extract from local poem, 83.
  poem " To a Daughter of New England," 84.
  Visit to Mr. Burton's library, 85-88.
  appointed appraiser of books, 89.
  illness and death, 90.
  conclusion, 90.
" Keese, John ; his Intimates," etc., preface, 39.
Keese, Jonathan Lawrence, 9, 9, note, 41.
Keese, Willets, 9, 41.
Keese, William, 7.
Keese, Wm. Linn, 1st, 8.
Keese, Wm. Linn, 2d, 41.
Kemble, Miss, 28.
Kent, James, 7, 20, 21, 23.
Kettell, ——, 31.
King, Charles, 21, 22.
Kossuth, Louis, speeches of, 15.

Lamb, Charles, 40.
Lawrence, Jonathan, Jr., 34, note.
Leggett, W., 34.
Lester, J. W., 79, 85, 86.
Lewis, Estelle Anna, 56.
Linen, James, 66.
Linn, Rebecca, 7.
Linn, Rev. William, 7.
Liston, John, 81.
Locke, Richard A., 21.
Longfellow, Henry W., 15, note, 33, 34, note, 40, 77.
Lowell, J. Russell, 40.
Lyell, Rev. Dr., 12, note.

Macaulay, T. B., 40.
" Major Jack Downing," 35, 44, 45.
Mellen, G., 34, note.
Mitchell, J. K., 34, note.
Mitchell, William, 31.
M'Lellan, I., Jr., 34, note.
Moore, Clement C., 34, note.
Morford, Henry, preface, 15, 38, 39, 80.
" Morford's Magazine," 39.
Morris, George P., 21, 31 ; auction-room story, 65, 66.
" Mourner's Chaplet, The," 35.

" Mulberry Feast " (story), 82.
Munden, Joseph S., 81.

Nathan, Jonathan, 12.
Neal, John, 34, note, 35.
Neal, Joseph C., 56.
Noah, Major, 21, 22.
" North American Scenery," 36.
Norton, A., 34, note.
Nott, Dr., address of, 14.

Oakes-Smith, Elizabeth, 34, 35, 58.
" Opal, The," 36.
Osgood, Frances Sargent, 47.
" Our Poets Forty-three Years ago," 33, note.

Paulding, James K., 20, 23, 34, note.
Peabody, W. O. B., 34, note.
Percival, James G., 34, note.
Pickering, H., 34, note.
Pierpont, John, 34, note.
Pinkney, E. C., 34, note.
Placide, Henry, 30, 74, 79, 85, 86.
Poe, Edgar A., 21, 24, 31.
" Poets of America, The," 22, note, 31, 32, 33, note.
Prentice, George D., 34, note.
" Prisoner of Chillon, The," 15.
Pritchard, William M., 12, note.
" Private Libraries in New York," 88, note.
Putnam, George P., 21, 25.

Read, Thomas Buchanan, sketch of, 55, 56.
" Rivals, The," performance of, 29.
Robertson, Anthony, 12.
Robins, George, 60, 61.
Rockwell, J. O., 34, note.
Rogers, Samuel, letter of, 24, 40.
" Rosalie Clare " (song), 57.

Sabin, Joseph, 62, note.
Sands, R. C., 34, note.
Sargent, Epes, 34, note.
Schell, Augustus, 12, 12, note.
Sigourney, L. H., 34, note.
Simms, William G., 34, note ; sketch of, 49, 50.
" Skeleton in Armor, The," 15, note.
Smith, L. P., 34, note.
Smith, Mr. and Mrs. Seba, sketch of, 44-47.
Smith, Sydney, 26.

INDEX.

Sprague, Charles, 34, note.
Stace, Mary Leighton, 54.
Stone, William L., 21, 22.
Street, A. B., 34, note.
Strong, Oliver, 12.
Sutermeister, J. R., 34, **note**.

Taylor, Mary, **31, 79**.
Thackeray, W. M., **40**.
"Then," 30, note.
Thorpe, Thomas B., 56.
Timrod, W. H., 34, note.
Trumbull, Colonel, 20.
Tuckerman, Henry T., 34, note, 35 **note,** 38; sketch of, 43, 44; men**tion,** 58, 59.

Van Winkle, E. S., 12, note.
Verplanck, Gulian C., 24.

Wallack, James, **85, 86**.
Webster, Daniel, **24**.
Webster, Noah, **24**.
Wells, A. M., 34, **note**.
White, Richard Grant, sketch of, 53, 54; mention, 58; **story** told by, 67, 68.
Whittier, John G., 34, **34, note**.
Wilcox, C., 34, note.
Wilde, R. H., 34, note.
Willets, Elizabeth, 9.
Willets, Zebulon S., 9.
Willis, N. P., **24**, 34, note; sketch of, 54, 55.
"Wintergreen, The," 36.
Woodworth, Samuel, 34, note.

"Yesterdays with Authors," 78, note.

THE END.

www.ingramcontent.com/pod-product-compliance
Lightning Source LLC
Chambersburg PA
CBHW021949160426
43195CB00011B/1285